The World of the Anthropologist

The World of the Anthropologist

Marc Augé and Jean-Paul Colleyn

Translated by John Howe

Oxford • New York

English Edition
First published in 2006 by
Berg
Editorial offices:
1st Floor, Angel Court, 81 St Clements Street, Oxford, OX4 1AW, UK
175 Fifth Avenue, New York, NY 10010, USA

First published in France, 2004 by Presses Universitaires de France
© Presses Universitaires de France, 2004, *L'Anthropologie*

This English translation © Berg, Oxford International Publishers Ltd

This work is published with the support of the French Ministry of Culture –
Centre National du Livre

ii institut français

This book is supported by the French Ministry for Foreign Affairs as part of the Burgess
Programme headed for the French Embassy in London by the Institut Français du Royaume-Uni

Berg is the imprint of Oxford International Publishers Ltd.

Library of Congress Cataloguing-in-Publication Data

Augé, Marc.
    [Anthropologie. English]
    The world of the anthropologist / Marc Augé and Jean-Paul Colleyne ;
translated by John Howe.—English ed.
        p. cm.
    Includes bibliographical references and index.
    ISBN-13: 978-1-84520-448-8 (pbk.)
    ISBN-10: 1-84520-448-4 (pbk.)
    ISBN-13: 978-1-84520-447-1 (hardback)
    ISBN-10: 1-84520-447-6 (hardback)
    1. Ethnology—Philosophy. 2. Ethnology—Methodology. I. Colleyn,
Jean-Paul, 1949- II. Title.

    GN345.A8413 2006
    301.01.—dc22

                                                                2006010292

British Library Cataloguing-in-Publication Data

A catalogue record for this book is available from the British Library.

ISBN-13   978 184520 447 1 (Cloth)
           978 184520 448 8 (Paper)

ISBN-10   1 84520 447 6 (Cloth)
           1 84520 448 4 (Paper)

Typeset by JS Typesetting, Porthcawl, Mid Glamorgan
Printed in Great Britain by the MPG Books Group, Bodmin and King's Lynn

www.bergpublishers.com

Contents

v

Introduction

The term 'anthropology' designates the study of
humanity in general. It is subdivided into physical
anthropology – the study of humanity in its biological aspect – and social and cultural anthropology. It
is the latter that concerns us here, dealing with the
ways in which language and economic, social, political and religious organization develop over time.
Given the impossibility of comprehensive detailed
coverage of this vast field in a work of this length, we
have decided to base it on a particular conception
of anthropology which is both classical and modern.
Classical because the theories of the past – and their
errors – have taught us things; modern because it is
a discipline that seeks its explanations freely, rather
than receiving ready-made ones from some traditional fount of authority.

We would like to help show that the methods,
observations and analyses of anthropology can help
explain the complexity of a contemporary world

subject to contradictory developments, a proliferation of diversities coinciding with the abolition of barriers. The contribution of anthropology rests firstly on a privileged methodology: prolonged research in the field, participatory observation, direct communication with social subjects who have their own interpretations of the world. It rests secondly on anthropology's epistemological fecundity, based on a history which is also that of its theoretical concepts and hypotheses. The study of that history, with its extensions into our contemporary areas of concern, is essential, because all the human sciences repose on anthropological presuppositions, usually implicit, which can only be brought to light by an effort of analysis.

This book – whose aim is to be practical – attempts to provide the reader with tools that can help him or her to understand the diversity of the present world. The goal may appear simple, but the road to it is nevertheless strewn with pitfalls: the vast quantity of published material, difficulties with vocabulary, the hermetic nature of some specialized works. The specialist pays little attention to questions put by the 'ordinary public', so little indeed that in a popularizing work it is difficult to 'translate' the more abstruse texts without trying to make them correspond artificially with the expectations of lay readers. Anthropologists rightly believed that a

2

specialized vocabulary needed to be developed, but on many definitions they have not managed to establish real consensus. The unprepared reader, hurrying to assimilate some aspect, may well become aware of a measure of disarray, but such apparent incoherence is really in the nature of conceptual reflection. Yesterday's big theories containing definitive truths were merely utopian. We could say that today the image of a key that opens every door has been replaced by that of a toolbox in which the researcher rummages at will, modifying the chosen instrument if necessary, to advance through a series of approximations. In practice, a specific piece of research nearly always leads to some reconstruction of the concepts adopted, to make them correspond with the subtleties of the facts as observed. This constraint is not the only factor making initiation to anthropology difficult. Not only has the number of published texts exploded over the last few decades, but it is also often necessary to refer to material from other disciplines, so true is it that anthropology is itself a 'crossroads' discipline. Most of the terms used by anthropologists are also used by everyone else. They are never 'purely academic' or 'purely technical', and often have an ideological connotation. It should also be noted that journalists make wide use of a sort of parody of anthropology, loosely employing exotic notions in an ironic way to designate a role or attitude in our own society: for example, one might see mentioned the 'sheikh of the Collège de France', the 'caste of Enarchs',[1] political 'pundits' on current affairs television, etc. Finally, while the tendency to specialized fragmentation continues to grow, the external frontiers of anthropology are becoming blurred, especially where they touch on sociology. The anthropologist is led to use the quantitative methods of sociology and sociologists often use the qualitative methods favoured by their anthropologist colleagues. Both attempt to understand the conception of the social world that its actors develop for themselves. Sociology has undergone something of a renewal through localized studies using the qualitative methods of ethnography. Some sociologists are very close to anthropology; and some anthropologists are changing fields, moving from Africa or the Amazon basin to Europe. It is from the meaning the actors assign to the objects, situations and symbols surrounding them that they fabricate their social world. There is another point of convergence: the social construct is not identified as a stable object, as it was by the first ethnographers whose objective was to validate traditions, but as a

1. Translator's note: an 'Énarque' is a graduate of France's élite École Nationale d'Administration or ENA.

collection of processes which evolve continuously through human activity.

It is no easy matter to distinguish what needs to be read from what may just be peripheral, given the enormous mass of books and papers. Whose opinion counts most? That of the academic world? Public opinion? Obviously the most frequently quoted texts have to be given proper attention, but unknown texts, ones that have passed unnoticed or been forgotten, are not necessarily to be despised. Posterity is itself a misleading teacher, for the specialized literature is forever turning up works that were neglected under the prevailing criteria of their own time.

The art of writing a miniature encyclopaedic work (if we are permitted this oxymoron) boils down to the issues of balance and scale. If we stay on the level of generalities, we lose the specificity that makes the anthropological approach worthwhile; if we linger over a particular case, we may not be able to see the wood for the trees. A book of this type should survey what its authors believe to comprise the shared knowledge of specialists, explain their more important divergences and at the same time eliminate false problems or blind alleys. The term *knowledge* is itself a subject of debate. The philosopher Gaston Bachelard warned against the classic form of popularization, and its tendency to pass on only results regarded as proven and established values. Our task here is not so much to identify a common heritage or provide insight into the different cultures of the world, but rather to try to suggest a few intellectual tools to facilitate comprehension of these things. It is out of the question for us to map the entire anthropological field which embraces the human condition in its entirety. So this short book will be neither a dictionary nor a *Who's Who*, since in such a small number of pages the enterprise must consist of highlighting a few names and neglecting the others. In all honesty therefore we have no choice but to feature our preferences, while allowing other voices to be heard.

1

Understanding the Contemporary World

I CONFUSION OVER TERMS

Ethnography, ethnology, anthropology: the confusion of these terms, in the academic literature as well as in popular writings, can mislead the reader at the outset. So let us try briefly to sort them out. Ethnography originally designated (late nineteenth and early twentieth centuries) the description of the habits and customs of so-called 'primitive' peoples, ethnology the encyclopedic knowledge that resulted from it. Broadly speaking, ethnology appeared to be the branch of sociology devoted to the study of 'primitive' societies. At that time, the word 'anthropology', on its own, was still reserved for the study of humanity in its somatic and biological aspects. Even today, in the United States, 'anthropology' used on its own usually means the study of human biological evolution and cultural evolution during human prehistory. A lot of university departments there still group physical anthropology with archaeology and cultural anthropology. But since the end of the nineteenth century, the expression *cultural anthropology* has designated the comparative study that can be derived from ethnography and ethnology, conceived respectively as the collection and systematic analysis of data. British authors, on the other hand, prefer the expression 'social anthropology' to 'cultural anthropology', because they favour the study of social acts and institutions.

During the 1950s Claude Lévi-Strauss introduced the anglophone term 'anthropology' (but without the qualifying adjective 'cultural') to denote the study of human beings in all their aspects. As it had in the United States, the word demoted – but did not wholly replace – the term 'ethnology'. The success of structuralism and its impact on the other human sciences, on the one hand, and the links of anthropology with philosophy and sociology, on the other, have led to a situation in France today in which 'anthropology', used on its own without qualification, means the discipline that deals with the current diversity of human cultures. This usage offers the advantage of greater objectivity by superseding the idea of a closed domain consisting of primitive societies fixed in a static history, with no destiny but to reproduce themselves identically or die out. We should note, however, that the abandonment of the ethnocentric approach – classifying the races and then the ethnic groups or societies according to criteria that assumed the supremacy of Western civilization – has managed to rehabilitate the term 'ethnology'. Renunciation of the 'primitivist' category has sometimes justified extending the use of the term 'ethnology' into the so-called 'modern' world, with ethnology now being conceived as theoretical study based on small-scale research, the researcher's prolonged immersion in the field, and participating observation and dialogue with the informants. That is why we sometimes see references to urban ethnology, industrial ethnology, family or neighbourhood ethnology, and so forth.

To finish with this square-dance of names – whose complexity we have barely sketched – let us recall that anthropology as the science of humanity embraces both physical anthropology and social and cultural anthropology. The latter, a synonym for ethnology, applies to all human groups whatever their characteristics. It can take as an object of study any social phenomenon that needs to be explained through cultural factors.

II THE STAKES OF ANTHROPOLOGY

Unlike most animal species, humanity is not linked to a specific environment: the whole planet is available to it and it is by means of culture that it adapts to very diverse surroundings. Because of its biological determinations, it is capable of a vast range of different comportments, developing as it does not only in a natural environment but through a long upbringing in particular social and cultural surroundings. It is a banality to say that man is a social animal, but the methodological consequences should be understood: the human condition can only be envisaged in terms of social organization. Anthropology has demonstrated the intimate solidarity between the individual body and the social relation, the impossibility of thinking about sickness and death in purely individual terms. It is similarly impossible to think of man as solitary; man thinks of himself only in the plural. All human thought is social, and all anthropology is therefore also sociology. The apprenticeship in routines, the acquisition of habits that become ingrained in minds and bodies, relieve human beings of having to reflect and take decisions all the time. Quite a lot of our behaviour, while not being subject to conscious representation, nevertheless obeys rules and conforms to an appropriate way of conducting ourselves in society. The meaning is implicit and not represented. These automatisms liberate human beings and make them capable of innovation, but they can become a burden over time, evolving more slowly than the context and falling 'out of synch' with it. Anthropology studies

the intersubjective relations between our contemp-
oraries, be they Nambikwara, Arapesh, adepts of a
Brazilian Candomblé cult, Silicon Valley yuppies,
citizens of new towns, company bosses or Euro-
MPs. These relations of otherness and identity are
not given once and for all but are in constant recomposition. Language, kinship and matrimonial
alliance, social and political hierarchies, myths,
rituals, representations of the body, all express the
incessant effort of all societies to define selfhood
and otherness. How, in a given setting, is the relation
between one group and another seen by each group?
This is the specific object of anthropology, for this
relation necessarily takes on a meaning, exposes
relations of force, is symbolized. Whatever the
theoretical leaning of the researchers, the specificity
of the anthropological viewpoint lies in this central
interest in examining the relation with the other as
it is constructed in its social context. The question of
meaning – in other words, the means through which
the human beings living in a social space reach
agreement on the way to represent it and act in it
– is the horizon of the anthropological approach.
This question also lies at the heart of current
philosophic debate, which could be described as a
tension between particularism and universality. No
doubt the first generations of anthropologists may
have exaggerated the internal coherence of cultures

they saw as more homogeneous than they really were, but the configurations corresponding to a particular culture or society are not totally arbitrary in origin. Anthropologists find patterns there, and by comparing them with others can theorize these different elaborations of meaning. They may, for example, find a nomenclature for the degrees of kinship among the Samo of Burkina Faso that has already been identified among the Omaha Indians of North America, or compare different forms of royalty that have existed in different times and places.

There has been much discussion of the notion of otherness which, owing to the 'exotic' beginnings of the discipline, may have seemed a constituent element of the anthropological approach, but really it is more a question of the researcher's own mental attitude, involving the exercise of systematic astonishment in investigating social acts. The exercise is probably easier to practise *in a foreign setting*, but this systematic astonishment is focused more on the anthropologist's own impressions and interpretative leanings than on the effect of strangeness produced by the behaviour of the others under examination. The researcher must constantly question his own a priori and adopt a learning posture. He is forced to do so in any case, even close to home, when working in an unfamiliar milieu. The ethnographer therefore has to manage two contradictory postures: to avoid overlaying his observations with preconceived ideas stemming from his own culture, while maintaining a certain distance from the observations in order to range them alongside information arising from other contexts. The notion of otherness is central to the anthropological approach, not so much because anthropology deals with diversity, but rather because otherness is its instrument. A research project necessarily implies the existence between the observer and his object (the people he or she is 'studying') of a gap that has to be managed. One has to avoid generating exoticism by selecting only the juiciest indices, but, inversely, it would be absurd to preach confusion between analyst and object. It is no longer enough these days to familiarize ourselves with what seems curious at first sight, or to discover the strangeness lurking in our own most ingrained habits, for a crisis of meaning is affecting the entire planet and this crisis has resulted in the explosive proliferation of quests for identity. At a time when information flashes round the planet at electronic speed, when exoticism itself is becoming a consumer product or even a political asset, every individual is violently confronted with the image of the world. The concept of the human individual and relations between humanity and its environment could not remain unaffected by such jolting developments as chemical agriculture, antibiotics, genetically modified plants and animals, genetic medicine, DNA research, cloning, hormone treatment, organ transplants and test-tube conceptions. Since time immemorial, people all over the world have been interested in differences of language, usages, customs and mores, but today, on planetary level, they are becoming increasingly aware of their interdependence, and thus of their differences and the transformation of the world. They are producing a spontaneous anthropology, one whose goal is not knowledge but construction of an identity, perhaps even the expression of a political strategy. Less paradoxically than one might think, the process of globalization is being accompanied by a rise in political demands hinged on ethnic cultures or traditions. Individuals and institutions elaborate social theories that incorporate, more or less explicitly, the vocabulary and ideas of the human sciences, reconfiguring them when necessary to suit their causes. For the anthropologist, this proliferating discourse on identity – often hybrid, sometimes verging on the bizarre – is a new field of study.

Bachelard warned against the categories thrown up by common sense. These days they are projected, usually in uncritical fashion, by the press, which borrows promiscuously from every linguistic mode, political, artistic, social and scientific. Thus for example we read of a *resurgence of religion*, not long after the prediction of a disenchanted world; but it is clear that such new religious movements as Islamic integralism, or evangelism in Latin American and African countries, have little in common with religion as it presented itself before the 1960s. The journalistic expression 'The world of' fashion, finance, sport, etc. is inexact but conveys a sound intuition. It is inexact because these worlds are not really worlds: they are closely connected with one another. But it is right to place the shimmering reflections of these 'constructed' worlds in the mirror of a humanity more co-present with itself than ever before. Really there is no longer any such thing as a cultural isolate, since all the spaces occupied and symbolized by humanity are now being analysed in a global context. Between a quarter and a third of the world population watched the 1998 football World Cup on television. The standard of living of a Senoufo peasant in Mali is determined by the stock market price of cotton on the world market. A song recorded in South Africa by the Congolese guitarist Mwenda Jean Bosco becomes a hit 3,000 kilometres away in Sierra Leone. The lives of schoolchildren in Kingston, Jamaica, are profoundly affected by the rulings of the World Bank and International Monetary Fund. Nearly all the world's peoples have their living conditions determined by decisions taken elsewhere. They are subject to the economic, political and cultural dominion of foreign governments and external forces. Their lives are concretely affected by demographic, bio-medical, ecological, economic and political phenomena that escape their control but bring them together with other groups subjected to similar constraints. Be they peaceful (tourism, world music, cultural or artistic movements) or otherwise (shanty-towns, refugee camps, gangs, illegal immigration, drugs, prostitution), the new fields of anthropology are historical in nature and changing constantly before our eyes.

III THE CONTEMPORARY WORLD

Contemporaneity is defined by the fact of living in the same epoch and sharing common references. For many years ethnologists believed that they could travel through time by travelling through space, expecting to find the image of ancient societies in the Antipodes. That was a myth, but there is nothing intrinsically improbable in the idea that a particular society might have remained untouched by the general movement of the world. What is new today is that, whatever the mode of life of the people inhabiting our planet, there now exist shared references. We have our local landmarks, decipherable by our small milieu, but we also share a world culture backed by other references. For an anthropologist, the choice of research object and the methodology adopted imply a measure of immersion in a particular environment (the 'field'), but, at the same time, the study is not a simple matter of interpersonal relations *in situ.* Beyond the internal perspective, these relations find a second level of explanation in the study of external determinants: geographic, demographic, historical, political, institutional and other objective constraints. The meticulous description of human behaviour in its historical and cultural context, on the one hand, and its comparison with other forms in time and space, on the other, are the basis of the analytic capacity specific to anthropology. And for that very reason, anthropology ventures beyond its own definition in terms of objects and methods to open the way to a more comprehensive intellectual project. The confrontation of different models, norms, cultural patterns, fields of thought, and their comparison and discussion, are systematic ways of trying to visualize a human condition undergoing perpetual redefinition.

The anthropology of contemporary worlds recognizes the plurality of cultures, but also the references common to all of them and the internal differences present in a single culture. While the concept of culture still has a measure of operative value, it is no longer conceived as a body of knowledge all of which is shared by all members of the society

17

in question. Within a single society, rather, there coexist a plurality of forms, and the cultural baggage of its members varies according to social parameters (age, sex, education, wealth, profession, political convictions, religious affiliation, etc.). The notion of *acculturation*, so widespread in popular anthropology, to designate the range of phenomena resulting from the collision of two different cultures, is misleading in that it assumes that each body was pure and homogeneous in the first place. That of *hybridism*, more fashionable nowadays, is of little more use, indeed equally misleading with its biological connotation. Terms that are too general or too all-embracing often turn out to be fairly useless. While anthropologists need the term *society* to designate a group living under a common system, the term *system* can itself induce error if taken to suggest a perfectly integrated whole. Conflict and change are, in fact, constituent elements of any society. The adoption of a systemic perspective does not prevent variability and change, or the viewpoints of the actors, from being taken into account. Different perspectives are what anthropology needs. Two studies of the same object along different lines are not mutually exclusive, even though a researcher may not be able to carry them both out at once. When undertaking the study of differences and specificities, one should avoid the pitfall of isolating within a society, more

2

Objects of Anthropology

I FROM SALVAGE ETHNOGRAPHY TO GENERAL ANTHROPOLOGY

The discipline is changing, and so is its object. In its classical period anthropology favoured the study of small exotic societies, with reference to their immediate context. It was strongly influenced by *salvage ethnography,* whose priority was to describe the state of societies in the process of disappearing before the expansion of European civilization. Today, with the strengthening of economic and political interdependence, the spectacular increase in individual mobility and the even more remarkable acceleration in the circulation of messages, this immediate context extends to the entire planet. People, wherever they may be, are only local because of a particular historical configuration. How for example, given the increasing interdependence of the world system, can the Zulus of South Africa,

21

the Namibians, the Tutsis and Hutus of Rwanda,
the people of East Timor, the Nicaraguan Miskitos,
the Kurds, the Afghans, the Lebanese Shi'ites, be
seen as autonomous cultures or understood outside
the global context? The Nuer – that canonical
example of a society without a state – are in the early
twenty-first century entangled in a bloody civil war,
complicated by religious differences, for control of
petroleum resources between the southern Sudanese
populations and the Khartoum government. So a
group apparently little touched by changes in the
outside world is no longer in the situation of a
century ago: its enclosure or relegation results from
a particular political and economic – in a word,
historical – conjuncture. There are very few groups
left in the world that have no experience of working
for wages or machine-made goods. The Kayapo
Indians of the Amazon, wearing full ritual dress,
demonstrate in Altamira or Brasilia against violations
of their territory, recording their 'news' on video.
Resistance to Islam by the Kalash in the Hindu Kush
or the Dogon in Bandiagara is carefully managed
to preserve the tourist attractions of these regions.
Far from representing the permanence of a culture
opaque to change, these two groups only illustrate a
state of their societies at the moment of observation.
Combined with other methods, ethnographic
description would seem to be a necessary stage in

any serious study of the new phenomena resulting from the complex relations between contexts of domination and the concepts of minorities and political/cultural movements: Chicano and Zapatista in Mexico, pan-Mayan in Guatemala, black communities in Colombia, landless peasants in Brazil, rural workers at Porto Alegre, and so on. The current epoch confirms the evolution of anthropology, a gradual shift from the study of peoples to the study of themes. It would be wrong, however, to see this as a radically new development. Émile Durkheim and Marcel Mauss made no radical distinction between exotic domains and familiar ones. And they sought less to produce a detailed analysis of a particular society than to study such themes as magic, religion, the gift, sacrifice or the division of labour.

II DIVERSIFICATION OF DOMAINS

Such is the diversity of subjects interesting to anthropologists that we are witnessing an ever-increasing specialization, whose most visible sign is the proliferation of names: anthropology of childhood, of education, of war, of art, of sickness, of space, of development, of city life and even anthropology of anthropology. These appellations are usually thrown up for reasons of institutional convenience, but are quickly validated by use, so much so that it becomes pointless to contest or bypass them. It is appropriate, however, to understand these more or less new domains as different empirical objects, not as sub-disciplines. In the latter case, analysis might easily be reduced to a sort of amateur surgery adapted to specific domains – political, holy, religious, artistic – when really they are all necessarily interdependent. That is why we prefer, as the lesser of two evils, to talk about anthropologies of law, of religion, of sickness, of town life, and so forth, rather than using more closed categories such as juridical, religious, medical or urban anthropologies. This solution at least preserves the idea of a single anthropological aim: for it is only by taking the whole of humanity as its field of study that anthropology assumes its proper dimensions. Moreover, given the spectacular increase in the number of researchers and published papers, it has become impossible for a single reader to assimilate all of the anthropological 'literature'. Nevertheless, despite the obligation to specialize, it is crucial to try to maintain a generalist outlook and struggle against the ghettoization of learning. The current expression 'anthropology at home' is misleading: what it refers to is the study of social relations, essentially the same process whether the context is Western or exotic. When we are trying to describe some aspect of our European mode of life, we are careful not to force the information. We try to understand what the anthropologist's questioning might signify for the person being questioned. We thus conduct a critical analysis of the curious enterprise that consists in describing, and therefore writing down, the culture of other people, in a different geographical and historical environment. Anthropology strives to reach a truth carried, often unknowingly, by the people it interrogates. Here, as in the Antipodes, at least in the early stages of the enquiry, the anthropologist has to 'become a native' to comprehend the advantages and limitations of the anthropological project.

Let us move on to the custom of fabricating words based on the prefix 'ethno-', for example ethno-economics, ethnocentrism, ethno-cinema, etc. These composite words suggest that the domain, attitude or activity owes its characteristics to a specific culture or is focused in part on cultural factors. We also see the word 'ethnoscience', a term that is doubly ambiguous: ethnoscience is sometimes understood as a branch of ethnology, sometimes as the knowledge of other peoples in a particular domain and the comparative analysis of that knowledge, and sometimes yet again as the comparative study of a particular domain across different cultural groups. The term *ethnohistory* designates a branch of history (often practised by anthropologists) concerning societies without writing, to which classical historiography as such cannot be applied. A number of authors have criticized this appellation for giving scholarly endorsement to the reclassification of primitive societies in a separate category from the rest of humanity. *Ethnobotany* sometimes means the study of the plants used by the peoples studied by the ethnologist, sometimes the indigenous theory of plants. *Ethnomedicine* is sometimes the study of the medicine practised by 'others', sometimes of the others' theory of medicine, where there exists in the society concerned a separate domain that can be so described. Much the same can be said of history, psychiatry, musicology, and so on. It would undoubtedly be more productive to think in terms of angles, avenues or lines of research rather than of separate disciplinary fields. The anthropology of illness, for example, throws new light on some of anthropology's classical and less classical subjects such as the notion of self (Marcel Mauss), symbolic efficacy (Claude Lévi-Strauss), biopolitics (Michel Foucault), the coexistence of several cultures, immigration, etc. Lastly, ethnoscience has a third area of meaning that partly overlaps the other two: it designates the analysis, inspired by linguistics, of the classifications and procedures employed by different cultures in the domains of learning and its applications. This last, it could be said, partially overlaps the body of research covered by the term 'cognitive anthropology'.

Structural analysis had the merit of trying to throw light on the work of symbolic construction, the categories of understanding grasped before their 'domestication' by systematic, scholarly thought. Cognitive anthropology takes up and continues this effort by using rigorous methods to try to answer the question of how the natural world is constructed locally. On the subject of these domains designated by composite words based on the prefix 'ethno-', a separate case should be made of ethnomethodology, a tendency in American sociology which applies the methods of ethnology to the observation and analysis of everyday life. Harold Garfinkel and his associates start from the principle that every social group is capable of understanding itself, commenting on itself, analysing itself. Ethnomethods are the procedures that the members of a given society use to produce their world, to recognize it, to make it familiar. Calling them ethnomethods has the effect of marking these methods as belonging to a particular group, to a local organization or institution. Ethnomethodology thus becomes the study of the ethnomethods in daily use by the actors.[3]

3. See Alain Coulon, *L'ethnomethodologie*, Paris, PUF, 'Que sais-je?', 5th edition, 2002.

III CONSTRUCTION OF OBJECTS

The relation between thought and language poses problems which have yet to be resolved, doubtless a main cause of the indefatigable squabbling over words between scientists. We construct our objects of study by trying to define and analyse social facts that appear neither as natural species nor as empirical objects. But we are often obliged to proceed in two stages: first by making distinctions, in other words simplifying, then by reintroducing complexity. We can try to eliminate from our habits of thought such over-entrenched categories as *kinship, economics* or *religion*, but we are still obliged to take account of the specializations in specialized fields of research. Apart from that, since one has to classify in order to think and sort into chapters in order to explain, we are obliged to reintroduce global terms. But these divisions should be understood as being one of the principles on which information is structured. The reader will be careful to see them not as the proper names of distinct empirical objects, but as purely conceptual ordering arrangements. It is quite clear that the domains we are now addressing overlap one another in reality and are mutually entangled.

1 Kinship

An American author said a few years ago that the
analysis of kinship was to anthropology what the
nude is to art. Kinship and the rules of matrimonial
alliance are central to the study of the small-scale
societies which were the first object of anthropology.
In those societies, one cannot understand anything
to do with social relations without first analysing
kinship: relations between men and women, formation of social groups, relations between groups,
housing, land distribution, inheritance, concept of
the individual, relations with the ancestors, social
hierarchies, and so on. Inaugurated in the context
of societies that used to be called 'primitive', kinship
analysis has been extended to all the forms of social
organization, including societies officially based
on the management of social life by anonymous
bureaucracies, the market economy and personal
merit. All over the world, in fact, relations between
human beings are largely codified by kinship
structures, in other words connections of descent,
germanity (brother/sister relations) and alliance.
This codification is historical in nature, as can clearly
be seen in our own society with the emergence of
women's emancipation and new family configurations. Kinship is evidently social, and not biological
as we tend to think in Western societies, preoccupied

29

as we are with bonds of blood and genealogy. It would be difficult to argue that kinship and alliance no longer play any role in Western societies, whether in the world of business, spectacle or politics. It is obvious that market and contractual logic have not dissolved the social relations often described (after Max Weber) as 'traditional', or the mechanisms of social reproduction. The first theoretician of kinship, an American, Lewis Henry Morgan (1818–1881), when getting to know the Iroquois, had noticed straight away that a term used to designate or address a kinsman could also be applied to individuals occupying very different places in the genealogical tree and the chart of alliances. He suggested the notion of classificatory kinship, which is still in use today. To organize their social life, different human societies have imposed their own forms of order on the biological base. So it is necessary to study, case by case, the terminology of kinship, the rules of descent, of marriage, of residence. But these structures can be perceived in quite different ways. The clash between believers in the formal analysis of kinship systems (ironically denounced as 'algebra' by Bronislav Malinovsky!) and those focused on actual practices generated vigorous polemics. Some authors even maintain that kinship is an artificial domain and that kinship references cannot be separated from the other spheres of life, especially the economic and juridical. Heated debates have taken place between theoreticians of descent, who study the formation of social groups (nuclear family, extended family, lineages, clans, tribes, and so on) and those of alliance, who focus on matrimonial exchanges between groups. Kinship terminology is one of the domains giving eloquent proof that all human societies elaborate a finite number of comparable systems: how are the different classes of relatives addressed or designated? Anthropologists can determine the logical principles on which the main structural stereotypes of kinship terminology are based. These terminologies involve both the principles of descent (from what group?) and of alliance (married to whom?). All societies are up to a point endogamous (people marry their like), but all also follow an exogamous principle requiring people to marry outside the close family group. Definition of the degree of consanguinity prohibiting sex or marriage varies with different cultures, and is thus not prescribed by any natural law. In systems of matrimonial exchange a broad distinction is made between elementary systems, semi-complex systems and complex systems. In elementary systems a highly specific form of marriage is prescribed or advised; the choice of spouse is indicated by birth. For example, a man may be required to marry a girl classified as the daughter of his mother's brother; or a girl may have to marry into a lineage into which a sister of her father has married. In semi-complex systems, the interplay of prohibitions restricts the choice of possible spouses, until the model comes to resemble the elementary one. These systems specify the groups into which marriage is forbidden. Complex systems, on the other hand, proclaim freedom of choice, but this theoretical freedom is restricted in practice, fairly obviously, by sociological determinants (social origin, wealth, educational level, training, culture, geographical proximity, social pressures, etc.). Systems that require women to be 'bought' with the payment of a marriage indemnity (usually carefully calculated and codified in the form of prestige goods, so many head of livestock, lengths of cloth and/or other payments in money or kind) are generally complex systems. From a different angle, it could be said that that the exchange of women is here being mediated by the exchange of goods. Be that as it may, exchange lies at the heart of human societies, even though the rules vary enormously in detail.

Descent seems to us to be based on biology, but in reality it is also codified by culture. There is a link of descent between two individuals when one is descended from the other or when both are descended from the same individual. This rule determines the group to which the individual belongs. Descent is the principle that defines the transmission of kinship, assigns a status to each individual, defines functional groups. Certain concepts designate the social groups defined by kinship which, from a logical point of view, stack together like nesting furniture. Lineage groups people who consider themselves descended from a common ancestor and who can reconstruct their genealogy back to that ancestor. The terms patrilinear and patrilineal descent are used where the kinship line is transmitted through men and matrilinear and matrilineal descent where it is transmitted through women. The concrete groups one comes across in the field are often constructed on the basis of a lineage reference but also contain members of other lineages (most notably, of course, wives or husbands). Here one might use the term lineage groups. The lineage group as a concrete social unit has a size limit. Various material and social constraints may cause a lineage group to divide into segments. Sometimes, the leaders of these segments continue to maintain close relations in the name of their common origin. Sometimes, there remains only a vague sentiment of affiliation, and each segment, in reference to its own founder, becomes an autonomous lineage.

The clan is a group whose members consider themselves descendants of a legendary or mythical common ancestor, without being able (or willing) to reconstruct their precise genealogy. Each clan therefore contains a number of related lineages. The term patrilineal clan is used where the line of descent is transmitted through men, matrilineal clan where it is transmitted through women. In some societies, clan membership determines the whole of social life, the work done, as well as marriage, role in ritual events or military duties. In others the functions of the clan may be vaguer, and less important in daily life. In a patrilinear regime *ego*, the individual of reference (male or female), belongs to the group of his or her father, but a man and, for example, his sister's son, do not belong to the same group: the sister's son belongs to his father's group. A woman's children are not part of her kin but of her husband's. In a matrilinear regime, with kinship transmitted through women, *ego* belongs to the mother's group. A man and his brother's son, for example, do not belong to the same group: the brother's son belongs to his mother's group. A man's children are not his kin but his wife's. It is important to understand that in such a society, social status and inheritance pass not from a woman to her daughters but from her brothers to the brothers of her daughters. It is the mother's brother who exercises authority. In bilinear systems (also called double descent systems), the individual is bonded with some groups through his or her ancestry in the male line and with others through descent in the female line. *Ego* therefore

fulfils some social obligations and exercises some
functions through membership of the matrilinear
group, and others because of the connection with
the patrilinear one. Matrilineage and patrilineage are
two distinct entities, both fully experienced. Lastly,
under a regime of undifferentiated (or cognatic)
descent, descent through the male line and descent
through the female line are equally important. *Ego*
is thus descended from four grandparents, eight
great-grandparents, and so on. Everyone belongs to
groups of close relations that overlap one another.
This makes it impossible to constitute permanent
groups, unless only some ancestors are singled out;
other reasons connected with housing, individual
choice and specific events help narrow the range of
possibilities still further.

A very old polemic still persists today between the
partisans of a biological determinism (sociobiologists,
evolutionary psychologists) and partisans of a cultural
determinism. More recently, the gender impartiality
of a fair proportion of the classic studies of kinship
has been questioned simply by underlining the
incontestable fact that they reflect a male individual
of reference. Today the majority of specialists try to
surmount the binary opposition between formalism
and pragmatism: an interest in the principles of
codification is no reason to ignore history, everyday
practices, gender construction, religious practices

or power relations. Besides, almost everywhere, however vigorous the local traditions may be, it is a good
idea to cast an eye over the influence of the state
and control of the judicial apparatus. Ethnographies
of the administrative circuits, more or less all over
the world, would be very enlightening today. We lack
the space here to review all the basic notions and
research methods, let alone the different 'schools'
of kinship study, all of which are nevertheless essential to an elementary grounding in anthropology.
This is not negligible stuff: some of the themes
that come immediately to mind are matriarchy (an
ethnographic myth), incest (universal in principle,
specific in definition), sexual equality (all systems
are constructed from the starting point of sexual
difference), the atom of kinship (all known systems
are based on a small number of fundamental relation-
ships), descent, adoption (universal in one form or
another), divorce, and so on. Readers can consult on
this subject the work of Claude Lévi-Strauss, Louis
Dumont, Françoise Héritier, Francis Zimermann,
Christian Ghassarian, Jack Goody, Robin Fox, David
Schneider, and others.

2 Economy, environment, ecology

Western economic science as such could not be
brought to bear on societies that were hardly, or not

at all, integrated into the market economy. Where the economy was not functioning as an autonomous sector, it was difficult to talk meaningfully in terms of allocation of resources, profit, the law of supply and demand, sale, purchase, credit, prices, wages, capital, and so on. After the discovery, in different parts of the world, of spectacular ceremonies involving large-scale distribution and destruction of goods, the image of the 'savage' struggling for simple survival started to lose definition. Franz Boas in 1909, Bronislav Malinovski in 1922 and Marcel Mauss in 1924 inaugurated a theory of exchanges and the gift which considerably altered the perception of 'primitive' economies. It was noticed that in some societies exchange did not necessarily have an economic purpose, and could not be understood without an overall picture of the social organization. 'Primitive' economies gradually ceased to be defined in negative terms (low productivity, absence of surplus, savings, etc.), and non-mercantile forms of 'economic' competition started to come to light. In widely scattered places, *potlatch*-type ceremonies (so named by the Indians of the west coast of North America) had the function of asserting the status of the groups taking part and giving it public expression. They also had the effect of 'neutralizing' any surpluses from the economic point of view. Accumulation followed by a calculated redistribution appeared as one of

37

the modalities of the exercise of power. Mauss had already observed that in some societies 'to give is to demonstrate one's superiority; to accept without giving is to subordinate oneself'. Extensive use of the term 'gift' turns out to be misleading, as the services, exchanges and gifts concerned cannot be interpreted independently of the individual strategies and social statutes that determine them. Some of these exotic institutions like the *potlatch* and the *kula* seemed calculated to surprise management-obsessed European observers. The *potlatch* was practised by the Indians of the North American west coast. Among these groups of hunter-fishermen, individuals of high rank strove to maintain their status by making ostentatious and competitive gifts. 'If I, as chief, have made you a gift, you, as chief, should give it back to me, augmented by a substantial coefficient.' These jousts could even end with the spectacular destruction of goods. Comparable actions, at least in principle, have been observed in places very widely scattered over the globe. The Kula circle is a system of balanced exchanges between a large number of small islands off New Guinea. This system creates and strengthens long-lasting alliances. Necklaces of red seashells (*soulava*) circulate, in richly decorated canoes, in a clockwise direction, while bracelets of white shells (*mwali*) circulate from island to island anti-clockwise. The 'exchangist' communities themselves consist of groups of several islands, but these operations are individual and seem motivated by the quest for prestige: each chief has his own network of hereditary partners, and a precise account of the value of the different shells is maintained. Remarkably, the exchanges are obligatory and any hoarding subject to social sanction. The analysis of these ceremonial exchanges tended to overshadow other, less prestigious areas of production and exchange, but research projects in the field proliferated. Karl Polanyi and George Dalton gave a new direction to economic anthropology by underlining the diversity of systems of exchange. Since then, specialists have been distributed between two poles depending on whether they think that, all nuances aside, some sort of universal economic laws do exist, or whether they think that in many human groups, the characteristics of production are imposed by the prevailing social relations and symbolic interpretation of the world. Most societies that are not governed essentially by the market economy have no word to designate the economy as an autonomous sector. Exchange has almost become an object of study in its own right, probably under the structuralist influence of Claude Lévi-Strauss, who from 1949 onward treated exchange as the major dimension of social organizations. In this as in other domains most researchers have distanced themselves from the structuralist enterprise, even while recognizing their debt to it by taking more interest in the logic of social groups and less in the workings of the human mind. When people seek nowadays to compare different societies or different institutions, it is to isolate the mechanisms at work in them, rather than to discover the mental frontiers of the symbolic aptitude peculiar to the human species. Field studies document exchange/alliance/power relations with such precision that any generalization becomes more difficult, without however offering any comfort to the ultra-relativist line. In France, anthropologists who take an interest in the economic facts have often started from Marxist or Marxist-influenced theoretical premises, trying to articulate economics, kinship, politics and ideology into a global analysis. While relatively few authors lay claim to an economic anthropology in so many words, the number of published works on these issues is in exponential growth, for since the pioneering works were published most human groups have been swamped by or integrated into the world economy. Study of the production and consumption of food and goods must today take account of numerous papers concerning relations between humans and the environment, the history of technology, anthropology of nature and biological management.

At first, anthropological studies of relations between humans and their environment were determinist: it was thought that different societies and cultures owed their characteristics to the environment in which they had developed. Cultural adaptation followed the same logic as Darwinian biological adaptation. As field studies multiplied, following the methods preached by Boas and Malinowski, they quickly showed that differences in social organization and cultural characteristics could not be explained solely in terms of environmental constraints. Societies living in the same surroundings displayed strong differences and societies rooted in very different environments presented bothersome analogies. From the evidence, environmental constraints did no more than set limits. During the 1950s, nevertheless, the idea of a more or less direct causality linked to the environment enjoyed a second vogue initially under the name 'cultural ecology' (Julian Steward), later 'cultural materialism' (Marvin Harris). All cultural features – from technology to ritual, by way of habitat and kinship systems – were held to correspond with rational choices imposed by the demands of local adaptation. But the multiplication of meticulous ethnographic descriptions and even historical studies cast new doubt on the key role played by the notion of adaptation: human history is littered with examples of disastrous choice in this matter of adapting to the environment. During the 1960s, totalizing epistemologies, Grand Theory and linear causality were increasingly contested. Some anthropologists continued to seek a global order of regulation and proposed the notion of ecosystem. An *ecosystem*, a concept borrowed from biology, is formed by the sum of the relations of material exchange in a given environment. This model has the merit of recognizing that, if the environment acts on collective human life, human beings also act on their environment. Recent research seems to show that 'virgin forest' – in the Amazon, for example – is not as virgin as all that: very old traces of livestock raising, hearths and cultivated fields have been found there. In comparison with the generally accepted principles of the anthropological discipline, this approach has the characteristic of downgrading the notion of culture, which is no longer studied for its own sake, the question now being how exchanges are materially balanced. Other researchers, favourable to an *ethnoecology*, have preferred to concentrate on the need to understand the motives of the social actors when making decisions. During the 1970s and 1980s there was an upsurge in criticism of the modern myth of ideal primitive societies, nomadic, isolated and living in symbiosis with their environment. Popularizing works, but also professional anthropologists, had contributed to the accumulation of this imagery by neglecting the history of contacts and exchanges. The polemic centred on the people dismissively

labelled 'the Bushmen' by European colonizers has
so far spawned more than 2,000 articles in learned
reviews, and is certainly not over. Controversies of
similar type have arisen over other hunter-gatherer
groups in Africa and Latin America. While we would
not wish to deny the pervasive influence of a sort
of romanticism even on the conduct of scientific research, what really emerges from all these arguments
is that local configurations are a good deal more
complex than was originally thought, making any
trenchant judgement difficult. More interesting
intellectually than the notion of adaptation – always
necessarily tautological – study of the diversity of
types of mediation between human groups and the
non-human world enables us to surmount such oversimplified contrasts as symbolism/practices, mean-
ing/function, idealism/culturalism/pragmatism.
This interest in the concepts of others led to what
has been called cognitive anthropology, based on the
ethnosciences, the scientific domains as perceived by
different cultures. As a formulation it is more neutral
and less backward-looking than such outmoded
expressions as *folk theories* or *indigenous theories*. At its
leading edge, cognitive anthropology comes close
to psychology, which it supplies with comparative
material, most notably from the study of child development. The agenda of cognitive anthropology
attempts to bring its scientific criteria to the same

level as those of the experimental sciences, but it
comes up against the same difficulties as cultural
anthropology in general: collection of information
in the field is never 'pure', but always inflected by
the researcher's hypotheses and particular interests.
By studying indigenous knowledge relative to
specific domains, these researches have considerably
enlarged the field of *what is interesting*: classifications,
reasonings, recall mechanisms, representations
relative to all the domains of knowledge. Cognitive
anthropology, to sum up, proceeds in the opposite
direction to the structuralist approach. Structuralism
starts from a body of very diverse social constructs
(kinship systems, myths, etc.) and reduces them, little
by little, to a few basic structures defining the mental
confines of thought. The cognitive approach, on the
other hand, starts from the mental mechanisms used
by the individual to think and act appropriately as a
member of a community. This leads it to take a close
interest in research on experimental psychology,
linguistics, logic and neurology (currently making
enormous strides). The question of (cultural) upbringing as it relates to cognitive capacities enables
concepts like socialization or acculturation to be fine-
tuned, or discarded as too vague. It is clear that if the
cognitive anthropology agenda were carried through,
if it managed to explain how beliefs are fixed, how
inference works, how memory is constructed out of

personal experiences, we would witness a spectacular convergence of the natural and social sciences. The opposition between nature and culture is in fact only a construct, since culture can be considered part of nature.

3 Anthropology of politics

The anthropology of politics sometimes looks like a means of assessing the whole field of anthropology rather than a specific object of study. This sets it apart, in the sense that the variability of forms of political organization has served as a typological criterion for the identification of social formations. Thought and analysis in this domain have long been obsessed by the wish to explain the genesis of the state, but the large-scale evolutionist typologies produced by Henry Summer Maine (1861), Lewis Henry Morgan (1877), Karl Marx (1859), Friedrich Engels (1884), V. Gordon Childe (1936) and Leslie A. White (1959), tracing the evolution of forms of social organization from the primal horde to the state, by way of the tribe and the chieftaincy, have not withstood their critics. The birth of an autonomous central power is never the result of a single universal cause: it may be associated with conquest, with the economic exploitation of one social class by another and the existence of a surplus, with control of armed force, with the need to organize production (for example through major irrigation works), with control of trade, etc. With a number of societies – think in particular of sacred kingship and ancestor worship – it is hardly possible to visualize the political level without first studying the religious bedrock. The European definition of politics (from the Greek *polis*: the city, the state), by limiting its meaning to the exercise of state power, left anthropology facing a residue of unexplained phenomena. Societies can be governed without a ruling class exercising, through a central government, real sovereignty over a well-defined territorial unit. One should avoid reducing politics to a simple question of power. The anthropology of politics bears far more on the construction and modalities of legitimate authority. While some precolonial societies had strongly centralized organizations based on an administration and coercion, others maintained their cohesion without a central power even being apparent. (These soon came to be called *acephalic* or headless societies.) Malinowski discovered that power could be expressed through the reciprocal play of services between the chief and the members of the group. Melanesian Big Men accumulate goods through their kinship and client networks, then reinvest them by giving competitive sumptuary feasts to officialize the support of their partisans. In some of the societies studied by anthropologists, the state and kinship may be closely interwoven. Matrimonial exchanges could play an important role in the extension of political networks. A chief or king may be able, with his economic privileges, to extend his network of allies by contracting numerous polygamous marriages. Societies lacking central institutions and in which relations between lineage groups are not regulated by a specialized authority, like the Nuer of Sudan, have been denominated *segmentary* societies. In these, the size of the political units in play depends on the fusion or opposition of the segments of lineages in relation to one another. In other societies, kinship groups are counterbalanced by age groups, hierarchized groups of individuals who all undergo the rites of socioreligious initiation together. Among the Kikuyu of Kenya, for example, the chiefs of senior age classes are the holders of political authority. Among the Ochollo of Ethiopia, current problems are dealt with in plenary assemblies. Moreover, the apparatuses of power often involve rituals and cosmological representations, and this makes the anthropology of politics inseparable from the study of representations. Marc Augé has suggested elsewhere the concept of ideologic to designate configurations that articulate both relations of power and relations of meaning. The institution of royalty often presents a sacred dimension: as the king is at the meeting point of the

divine world and the social one, his function appears
necessary to the perpetuation of the rhythms of
the cosmos and the success of the big annual ceremonies. In the event of lasting catastrophe, the excep-
tional nature of royal power renders it precarious.
Adversity, attributed to the king's excessive vigour
– or alternatively to his feebleness on account of
old age, illness or sterility – designates him the ideal
scapegoat. A power appears more legitimate if it
seems woven into the natural order of things. It owes
its effectiveness to general ignorance, partial at least,
of its underlying mechanisms. The order that stems
from it may be more or less explicit, and may not
lead to the articulation of juridical rules until their
violation has given rise to a sanction imposed by one
or more socially qualified individuals. Among the
Andaman of Sumatra, the only sanction that existed
was pressure of public opinion, brought to bear
through scoldings, sulkiness and mockery. Among
the Nambikwara of Brazil, in the 1930s when Claude
Lévi-Strauss was studying them, the power of the
chief reposed not on the constraint but the consent
of his subjects.

To understand all these mechanisms, politics needs
a definition broader than the one derived from its
etymology. The problem of the genesis of the state
has therefore given place to study of the diversity
of ways in which power is exercised, mechanisms of

domination, the means by which the state functions. Michel Foucault was doing an anthropologist's work when he drew attention to the diffuse forms of power generated by the institutions of biopolitics: health, hygiene, assistance policies, control of manpower flows, psychiatric and psychological institutions, criminology, prisons, asylums. The anthropology of politics also takes a particular interest in the different ways of producing territoriality, social stratifications, statuses and roles, the exercise of legitimate force and conflict management, and in relations between the law, rights of appropriation and politics. In these domains it is necessary to study not only the rules, but also practices which may be observed to contravene them. Social differentiations, whether based on gender, age, class, caste, division of labour or control of language, create and perpetuate forms of domination. In the analysis of these power distribution mechanisms a distinction is made (after Max Weber) between power and authority, the latter implying at least a measure of legitimacy. That is why every ideology seeks to appear innocent by basing itself on the nature of things. It will be recalled from Marx that the ideas that lead society are those of the rulers although, on the symbolic level, the dominated subjects may elaborate their own defence mechanisms. Community politics, for example, aims to extract a given social group or 'society' from its historical setting and protect it against the whole that contains it: in other words the state, suspected of assimilationism. Feminist postures are separated into two distinct lines: one asserts the specificity of the female gender with a right to be different, and contests male values; the other, exemplified by Judith Butler, maintains that there are no gender identities other than the ones imposed from outside by the state and by diffuse power structures.

That battle-standard of the post-structuralist philosophers, the study of discourse as a form of power, was eagerly taken up by all the social sciences including anthropology. From the 1970s on, the production of discourse became a favoured area for the study of power relations: who speaks the truth? Who has the right to speak? Who controls language? For a long time ethnographers sought to explain the mechanisms of power, politics and law in so-called 'traditional' societies without reference to the surrounding colonial or post-colonial politics. Under the colonial parasol, however, the power of some chiefs had been increased or reduced, or at any rate modified. An anthropology of anthropology also exposes the political dimension of relations between the observer and the observed. Protests against ethnographers have been occurring since the 1960s, most notably among indigenist movements in South America.

Violence is a major theme of the anthropology
of politics, but no general theory has suggested
itself so far. The range of work on this theme is extremely varied. Anthropologists may study how the
human body can become, for terrorist militants in,
say, Northern Ireland, Palestine or Sri Lanka, an instrument in the service of a cause. 'Dirty protests',
hunger strikes, suicide bombings are different forms
of this instrumentalization. Radicalization of posi-
tions in opposing camps determines physical commitment, taking action, the explosion of violence.
Political propaganda usually roots itself in history
and appropriates motives from the past to make a
montage, a modern mythology, which may (as it
did in Rwanda) result in a concrete programme to
exterminate the other. Anthropologically speaking,
the term 'war' would seem too all-embracing to cover
the actual diversity of situations. In the Melanesian
'world' alone we can distinguish between half a
dozen types of conflict. War can be institutionalized,
conventional, initiatory, economic; it can be civil,
military, customary or even established as a mode of
production. All war is, however, necessarily between
localized political units. The expression 'war on ter-
rorism' may have some value as a political slogan,
but anthropologically it is meaningless. While early
theories of social systems favoured a relatively static
vision, based on rigid ethnic typologies, they have

given place to analyses that underline both the historically constructed character of ethnic groups (notably through colonial law) and the eminently dynamic character of politics. One cannot assert that the object of anthropology is disappearing with the end of ethnicity and, at the same time, note the proliferation of *ethnic* causes. An ethnic group cannot in any case be compared with a natural species, which survives or becomes extinct. The production of ethnicity should be analysed as a historical phenomenon deserving close case-by-case examination. Static representations of cultural identity should be countered with the recognition that it is a construct, a process. Neither sociology nor anthropology can be satisfied today with the functionalist view that every constituent part of a whole society contributes to its overall equilibrium. In fact, although mechanisms exist in every society whose purpose and effect is to ensure cohesion, conflict and contradiction are also constituent elements. Since the 1960s, the collapse of the colonial empires and new political recombinations in a postcolonial or neocolonial setting have set the terms of new challenges for the anthropology of politics.

Europe specialists, after a period devoted to tracing vestiges of ancient folklore, have turned to the study of such burning but little-understood issues in democratic regimes as clientelism, inheritance

of functions and the links between local government and the state. Current world mutations – the
collapse of the Soviet bloc, globalization, multiculturalism, decline of the nation state and simult-
aneous resurgence of micro-states – have greatly
extended the list of concerns for anthropologists.
Multiculturalism, for instance, is a complex phenomenon in which the assertion of irreducible differences can be clearly observed, rubbing shoulders
with the principle of a more open society. While immigration into Europe, for example, leads to a sort
of *ethnicization* of the different immigrant groups,
the reason for this has less to do with any 'natural'
tendency that way on the part of the groups themselves than with a decline in the attractive power of
assimilation and integration. Politics is also the art
of administering and producing subjects, citizens. It
is therefore possible to decipher, from the different
measures taken in the social, public health, medical,
paediatric, geriatric, bioethical, security, educational,
and other domains, an implicit anthropology (in
the associated medico-moral politics) which the
researcher can bring to light and discuss in public.

Let us end with a remark on research ethics. The
anthropology of politics sometimes finds it difficult
to maintain a descriptive or explanatory attitude
devoid of such normative dimensions as social
criticism, political commitment, utopian longings,

defence of treasured ideals, predictions of the end
of history, and so on. There is a rival attraction: the
temptation to become an expert in the service of
institutions like NGOs and development agencies,
compelled to adapt and regenerate themselves more
or less continuously.

4 Anthropology of religion

The anthropology of religion should generally be
seen as belonging to a materialist tradition emancipated from theological interpretations, but it bears
nevertheless the durable imprint of the religions of
the book. Even atheist or agnostic Westerners find
it difficult to detach themselves from the idea of a
monotheist religion, linked to a text, exclusive and
therefore entailing conversion. It is hardly surprising,
given the complexity of the world, that human beings
in all latitudes should have sought to identify the
truths hidden behind everyday appearances. They
have formulated hypotheses on the energies driving
the world and often attempted to make the invisible
visible. It is obvious that Western thinkers, artists and
theologians included, do not have a monopoly of
notions such as energy, force, will, the soul, the vital
spark, the breath of life, and so on. They do not have
a monopoly of metaphysics, either in the sense of
seeking the causes hidden behind immediate appear-

ances or in the more academic sense of systematic speculation. The best ethnography proceeds not by recruiting privileged informants on themes like the gods, the ancestors or the faith, but by observing individual and collective practices and gathering a range of verbal and other information with a bearing on individual life in the process of being lived. 'Indigenous' theory is always caught in the act. Extrapolating from individual cases is always delicate. So it is essential, when taking that risk, to show how one is going about the task of reconstituting the whole body of beliefs with specific reference to such themes as the self, heredity, lineage, magic, etc. There is a considerable risk that the process of writing may close an open system in which the social actors rummage at will for solutions to problems of the day. The notions of faith and belief are especially difficult to handle in that, in a large number of contexts, religion seems coextensive with the culture as a whole. We know, after Michel Foucault and Paul Veyne, that several levels of truth can coexist in a single culture and even a single individual. A large part of 'religion' consists in mechanical observances and standard procedures for ceremonies, sacrifices and prayers. Until the 1960s, detailed descriptions of custom, belief, myth and ritual were usually employed in support of functionalist explanations: sometimes religious representations and practices were held to bolster social cohesion, sometimes they were held to reflect a vision of the natural and social world. The influence of Émile Durkheim's *Formes élémentaires de la vie religieuse* (1915)[4] counted heavily in this type of explanation. From this perspective, in effect, a religious belief is always true in so far as it fulfils a social function. For several decades, the idea was widely accepted that rituals express and reinforce group solidarity so systematically that the group is really worshipping itself. But today no one still thinks that a society can be envisaged as a homogeneous whole. The division between sacred and profane, crucial to the reasoning in *Formes élémentaires*, continues to cause arguments, as no consensus has ever emerged on a definition of the sacred. Marxist analysis, too, embraces a functionalist frame of reference, but has a supplementary dimension neglected by Durkheim: it perceives religion as an 'opium of the people', an ideological weapon in the hands of the ruling classes. A current neofunctionalist tendency visualizes religion more dynamically, in terms of the processes of legitimization of authority, expression of grievances by the ruled, class interests and individual strategies. In some contexts, ritual is presented as an extension of political struggle. Little by little, functionalist explanations gave place to theories that

4. Elementary forms of religious life (Tr.)

highlighted the construction of meaning, rituals being seen increasingly as vectors for information or as the expression of a particular view of the world. Claude Lévi-Strauss explicitly recognizes the fecund role of an article by Durkheim and Mauss, 'Les classifications primitives' (1903),[5] which drew attention to intellectual orderings of the world. Under the influence of linguistics, people were soon talking about symbolic codifications. All peoples, in effect, classify the animal and plant species, the elements and substances of nature, climatic phenomena, etc., into different categories. One of the hypotheses most discussed since the 1950s has been passed down to posterity under the name of the 'Sapir and Whorf hypothesis' (the authors being anthropologists and linguistics experts). According to them, there exists a necessary relationship between the categories and language structure and the way human beings apprehend the world. Thus, the language of the Hopi Indians would take a particular interest in movement, rather than the things that interest the European languages. For other authors, a large proportion of the cognitive processes takes place outside language. Structuralism, and also the theories of Gregory Bateson (*Towards an Ecology of the Mind*, 1973) in the United States, are memorable for affirming that, in

5. 'Primitive classifications' (Tr.)

orderings of the world, relations counted for more than actual objects.

Although ritual is not confined to the religious sphere, virtually no religion is without it.

The notion of *rites of passage*, originated by Arnold Van Gennep in 1909, had a considerable impact not just on religious anthropology but on all research concerning social organization. These rites, observed in specific phases, punctuate the life-cycles of individuals and structure society. The notion was taken up by many authors and has been reworked many times, notably by Victor W. Turner (*The Ritual Process*). It implies different stages of initiation, each accompanied by irreversible inscriptions on the body (scarification, sexual mutilations or other ineradicable markings). Quite often funerals, which sometimes initiate ancestor status, are regarded as the final rite of passage. In all cases, there is a need for meaning to be attributed to the fact that the individual body is finite while the collectivity or social body endures. Referring to Sigmund Freud, some authors have seen ritual practices as an expression of the initiates' internal conflicts. Freud himself searched through mythology and the ethnographic data of his time to buttress his theory of the unconscious. The universality of the Oedipus complex and the myth of the primitive horde, which Freud had revived, met with some opposition from anthropologists, but

Freudian principles exercised a powerful influence, at first in an oblique manner on the American so-called 'culture and personality' school, then more explicitly on Géza Roheim, Georges Devereux, Edmond and Marie-Cécile Ortigues, Roger Bastide and many other authors. The interest of this work resides in its attempt to articulate the individual level with the collective one. It goes beyond the idea of causality on the individual level: while religion does indeed often answer an individual's needs, it is not to satisfy their needs that the members of a given society are religious. Meanwhile, the discovery that in many cultures the individual is considered to be the ephemeral coming together of different elements, some of which pre-existed the individual and will survive his or her death, both enriched and challenged Freud's proposed structuring of the components of the personality. It is helpful to envisage ritual phenomena in the context of a sociology of mediations: the function of the ritual apparatus is to provide mediations necessary to the actions of humans on other humans. Behind the relations between humanity and nature or the gods, it is relations between humans that are being expressed and played out. The proclaimed recipients of the rites may well be gods, spirits or ancestors, but only as the mediators of a relation between human beings. In the final analysis the symbolic relation only connects humans. Rites resist classification as entirely religious, or social, or psychological, or aesthetic; they borrow from all these domains, something that doubtless explains their extraordinary seductive power.

Anthropology often comes up against problems of vocabulary, for it has to resist the wish to canonize its own conceptual definitions, while maintaining an attempt at rigour. Terms in the anthropological lexicon that help to fix the objects they are meant to describe are evidently too rigid. Others are too polysemous, requiring further qualification case by case, for example the words 'rites' and 'rituals'. For some authors, any repetitive and stereotyped action (the State Opening of Parliament in London, Dogon greetings, Balinese cockfighting) can be described as ritual. Ethologists who study animal behaviour in natural surroundings also use the word rites when discussing mating displays or codified attitudes of submission. For other authors, some reference to an invisible world (to a transcendent institution), participation by qualified priests and the intention to achieve something are essential to the definition of a rite.

Positivist ethnography, for the sake of convenience, used to talk of this or that people's religion as if it were a well-sorted doctrine that could easily be written down if required. Arbitrary distinctions were made between such domains as magic, sorcery and religion, when all are parts of a collection of codifications giving meaning to the natural and social world. This naïve catalogue did not withstand the assaults of structuralism and hermeneutics: the first drew attention to the work of symbolic construction and the categories of understanding; the second, in the form of an interpretative anthropology, tried to express social reality from the inside, raising new problems for field research and the writing process. Cognitive anthropology hopes to separate the study of religion from speculation and conceptual a priori by studying the principles that explain the genesis of beliefs. One of the difficulties it encounters is that it cannot easily make use of information assembled by other, less controlled methods. Any information that is advanced unaccompanied by very precise background data on how the author has gone about obtaining that result renders analysis of cognitive processes at work extremely fragile. At the present moment, religious anthropology masks under a single heading a profusion of different approaches, stemming from, on one hand, the diversity of cultures and, on the other, the diversity of work being done in other disciplines. In fact, the very autonomization of the 'religious field' continues to fuel debate, for it seems to fit comfortably into the broader set of the modes of thought. The notion of the supernatural is not universal; it imposed itself in Western civilization along with the concept of natural science. The domain of nature, observable by scientific methods, was counterbalanced by the domain of the imaginary, of myths and superstitions. The West as a result has had some difficulty in dealing with the irrational part of humanity. It just about manages, thanks to artists, some philosophers, psychoanalysis and the other forms of rationality suggested by anthropology.

5 Anthropology of performance

Anthropology reached a turning point at the end of the 1970s when, from being essentially a science of facts, norms and structures, it became a science of processes. Ethnic groups, cultures and their major public manifestations now appear less as closed, finished entities than products of history in a continuing state of flux. In all areas of the art of using the human body, Mauss believed, the ways imparted by upbringing are predominant. The notion of *habitus* (borrowed from Aristotle by Mauss and remodelled by Pierre Bourdieu) is aimed at identifying what is thus established, built into bodies and minds in the form of lasting predispositions. These pre-dispositions can be seen in postures, movements, mimicry, expressions of feeling, artisanal skills, the body's routine habits, 'the presentation of self in everyday life' (as Erving Goffman memorably put it). A large part of social life and of the cognitive processes is therefore not mediated by language, and may consequently be difficult to express in words. This simple fact argues strongly in favour of using photography and audio-visual recording alongside the methods of classical ethnography. In the case of spectacular public displays, films have revealed important aspects that are not linguistically constituted. The fact that the actors are engaged in 'representation' does not necessarily mean they understand all the implications of their playing. The British game of cricket as reinterpreted by the Trobriand islanders, or the Hawka genie cult filmed in Niger by Jean Rouch (*Les Maîtres-fous*, 1954) guy colonialism, but without any conscious satirical intent on the part of the 'actors'. They play sincerely with what is on their minds, without having the professional distance essential to what Diderot called the actor's paradox. A number of writings have drawn attention to the 'spectacular' dimension of social life. A whole vocabulary has permeated the human sciences: theatricality, production, play, act, gesture, drama, performance, role, sequences, etc. In the works of Michel Leiris, Erving Goffman and Victor W. Turner, these notions have been articulated into a proper theory that improves our comprehension of social life. However, we should beware of the over-interpretation that might be encouraged by resorting to theatrical metaphor too hastily (on the level of description) or too indiscriminately (on the level of interpretation). The English-speaking countries have established an interdisciplinary field called *Performance Studies*, sometimes imperfectly rendered in French as 'anthropology of the arts of spectacle'. In fact it is a much wider domain, embracing activities such as theatre, music and dance, as well as rituals, prayers, sacrifices, oral traditions, carnivals, etc. This type of analysis was inaugurated by literary criticism – theatre criticism to be exact – but anthropology was soon needed as parallels started to be drawn between theatricality and ritual. In both cases the event is intended to produce effects on the (often participating) audience. Communication with another world – an invisible world of ancestors or gods – is less through discourse than through evocative scene-setting that makes ritual converge with art. Anthropologists have almost always viewed rituals only in terms of their social effects, ignoring their aesthetic dimension although it is undoubtedly the main source of their effectiveness. Art used to appear as a source of information on the values, world-vision and ideology of a society, rather than on anything aesthetic. However, analysis of indigenous categories linked to ritual does bring to light issues of an aesthetic order. Every religion, every ritual needs beauty, staging, spectacle. 'Aesthetic' should not be taken only to mean the setting of art objects at a distance for purposes of contemplation but, on the contrary, the fact that ritual also plays on exploring the chasms in human consciousness, relations with the world, the cycle of life and death, the mystery of childbirth, the succession of generations, trials of strength between the living. When, in the darkness of night, the weak glow of a straw fire outlines one of the most secret African 'masks' raising its terrifying jaws towards the sky, there is an emotional effect on the initiates. Its dance is based on the alternation of appearance and disappearance, of the near and the far, of departure and return. Ritual choreography plays on the instability of forms: the apparition is barely glimpsed, something like a hallucination or a fantasy. The experience of the adept is never only visual; it is enthusiastic by nature. He dances, sings, shouts, heckles or responds to the god. This scene-setting of the hardly visible – when the bush spirits come into the village and the frontiers between the living and dead become blurred – contrasts with the well-meaning aesthetic of entertainment spectacle. Translating the English word 'performance' as 'spect-acle' causes loss of the 'performative' dimension (first brought to light by the linguists), which holds that the object (utterance, spectacle) and its creation are confounded; they occur simultaneously. Ritual spectacles are also 'performances' in the sense that whenever they occur they surpass themselves, or risk everything, however exact and detailed the standard procedures and prescriptions may be. Those spectacular events that serve as social media, the great collective rituals, carnivals and masquerades, are thus neither the reflection nor the illustration of a culture; on the contrary, they belong to the body of practices through which a culture creates and transforms itself.

Division into chapters such as kinship, economy, government, or religion may have a certain analytic utility, but it still breaks up the experience of the *total social fact* (Mauss) in which these chapters are all confounded. It is only by studying the productions put forward by the people themselves that a researcher can comprehend their relation to the world.

6 Ethnographic film and visual anthropology

When cinema was invented, quite a lot of scientists immediately wanted to use this new instrument to study humanity and observe and record its behaviour. In any case, anthropology and cinema appeared at almost the same time, making them as it were childhood friends. The public successes of fiction cinema soon made people forget that for quite a long time documentary output had predominated over works of the imagination. Today the documentary is over-shadowed by 'big cinema', but from time to time it can still achieve a remarkable breakthrough despite the saturation of the world in commercial images. The Lumière camera/projector, the 16mm format, synchronized sound, video and digital camcorders were all revolutionary technological advances favouring the development of lightweight equipment. This is an essential parameter for ethnographers, always anxious to prevent their presence in the field from being invasive and to avoid polluting the scenes they want to film. Today, using a digital camcorder the size of a snuffbox, an ethnographer can discreetly film the social situations he is observing and retain images of professional quality. The much-used category 'ethnographic film' is somewhat misleading since it also covers film shot by explorers, travellers, independent film-makers and television journalists. The images shot by the camera operators sent all over the world to film exotic scenes by commercial companies like Lumière, Pathé and Edison are often cited as early examples of ethnographic film. In current usage, despite repeated efforts at correction, the exotic paradigm continues to serve as a marker and common denominator. It must be admitted, too, that the films shot by professional ethnographers are often disappointing. It is understandable of course that as scientists, these 'film-makers by duty' may be

suspicious of the artifices of professional cinema. But
it is also true that until quite recently they tended
to profess a thoroughly naïve positivism, seeking
an illusory neutrality while ignoring the historical
and cultural determinants conditioning their own
gaze. Films were offered as faithful reflections of a
univocal reality; as if the 'real' could be reproduced
in a perfectly mimetic fashion unaffected by the gaze
brought to bear on it. The lesson came from professional film directors, Vertov, Flaherty, Grierson, Vigo,
Epstein, Ivens and others. Their purpose was more
artistic and social than scientific, but they had the
art of advancing a point of view. Some resorted to
manipulative techniques unacceptable to academics,
but they had the merit of knowing that the real does
not speak all by itself, that the observer edits reality
and constructs a discourse. They knew that historical
events – events that are not invented by a director
and actors – nevertheless have to be narrated, and
that the narrator is inevitably part of the story. This
was understood by Jean Rouch, who made numerous
ethnographic films in a very descriptive vein but
who, in other films, broke the documentary mould,
influenced the French nouvelle vague films of the
1960s and anticipated the major debates on reflexivity
in anthropology that took place in the 1980s. He
helped belie the image of dull, boring ethnographic
films, unimaginatively shot and accompanied by

tediously learned commentaries. Nevertheless, the expression 'ethnographic film' or 'filmic approach to ethnography' should be defended, because there is a method there. On the other hand, the expression 'anthropological film' verges on the absurd, because if what it means is films dealing with humanity then all films are anthropological and all films are sociological.

Visual anthropology, then, groups three types of activity: ethnographic field research based on the use of audio-visual recording techniques; the use of these techniques as a mode of writing and publishing; and lastly, the study of image in the broader sense (graphic arts, photography, film, video) as a research object. So not every specialist in visual anthropology becomes a film-maker, any more than every specialist in iconology is compelled to become a painter or engraver. As for the production of images as an object of study, anthropologists can no longer assume that the members of a society think and act exclusively in terms of cultural references that are ethnic, simple and homogeneous. We should not forget that cinema has existed in Brazil and India since its invention. For better and worse, all the peoples of the Earth are exposed not only to missionary proselytisms but also, on a much bigger scale, to messages that detach them from the strictly local level: radio, cinema, television, music clips, advertising, Internet. In the

course of life, the individual calls on a shifting complex of models and references from widely varied
horizons, from the profoundly local and deeply
rooted in time to the most volatile and ephemeral.
Only a study that gets to grips with the ethnomethods deployed by individuals in the course of
their daily lives (as Harold Garfinkel would say) can
enable us to understand the references, the acquired
dispositions and interpersonal strategies in a given
milieu. In this respect, the job of an anthropologist is
really the same whether he is working among Bororo
Fulanis in Niger or new-rich Silicon Valley computer
nerds. An anthropologist who sets out to make films
should first acquire the proper means. It is not an
activity to undertake in a dilettante spirit, 'above the
market', as a sort of accessory meant to illustrate
work the bulk of which is to be found elsewhere. For
a film-making anthropologist, the underlying reality
cannot be arbitrarily separated from the form, and
the job necessarily entails an artistic dimension. In
this connection, one needs to be emancipated from
the exclusively verbal models of writing. The effects
of knowledge are not conveyed through content
alone, but also through sounds, images, techniques
and style. Like a writer, the documentary maker
is careful with syntax, seeks the right expression,
works over the rhythm, the narrative, the emotion:
in a word, the *style*. Making documentary films is

a discursive art that involves hundreds of options: selecting significant details from reality, leaving others in the shade, framing, cutting, assembling, restructuring, balancing colours, mixing sound, and so on. The film-maker mobilizes a rhetoric specific to the work, locates interesting characters and situations, maintains unity of time and place or moves about, narrates a realistic linear chronicle or offers what Eisenstein called an 'intellectual montage'. Film and video excel at showing places, spaces, testimonies, standpoints, attitudes, postures, social interactions, fragments of life. Although, since every film is constructed, the dividing line between fiction and documentary may be blurred, the narrative pact offered to viewers by the film-maker is not the same in the case of an invented work as in that of a reality being addressed from a particular point of view. In the first case, creation covers the whole of the cinematic object; in the second, it bears on the processing of an object that can be understood in a thousand different ways. These days, no doubt thanks to technical progress, nearly all anthropology students preparing for their first field studies have the intention of 'filming', although not always with a very detailed plan. Unfortunately, supervision and training are not much in evidence. Teaching of the culture of the image remains underdeveloped, marginal and full of gaps; unlike books (in Europe at least), films are not circulated, or rarely, and even the great documentary classics are difficult to find. And in practice, students find it hard to conduct a classical ethnographic study, itself very demanding in time and resources, at the same time as an audiovisual project. Some, who are gifted where image is concerned, are led to abandon research and an academic career to make documentaries. It would be useful if the majority of new anthropologists were provided with sufficient audiovisual culture to enable them to make their own documents, or to collaborate knowledgeably with specialists. Where outlets are concerned, one must also deplore the adoption by television of an almost exclusively commercial logic which handicaps documentary output. Despite all these obstacles, production of films concerned with the human sciences is increasing spectacularly, and the quality of films by anthropology and sociology students has improved considerably in recent years. An interesting reversal should also be noted: the people who used to be the 'subjects' of ethnographic films are turning increasingly to the production of their own images and the documentation of their social life. Strategic use of the media by 'indigenous peoples' enables them for the first time in history to control their own images and send the messages they want to the international community.

7 Applied anthropology

Today, anthropologists are increasingly involved as consultants in studying such 'problems for society' as bioethics, the implications of new techniques for medically-assisted procreation, biotechnology, education, corporate culture, delinquency, religious sects, and so on. Applied anthropology comes up against a variety of constraints. Analysis of the logic of social situations is of interest to managers only if it can help them to adopt a position, state a doctrine and suggest measures. In general, decision-makers demand 'instant science' to help them adjust their choices to the very short term. A priori, this time constraint is in contradiction with the slow impregnation methods practised by anthropologists. However, a large number of studies show that this is a challenge worth taking up. The vast building site of economic development is still stalled despite all efforts. The Asian examples of spectacular economic take-off owe little to development 'strategies' and much more to movements of global capitalism and geopolitics. Very schematically, it might be said that the theorization of development has passed through stages dominated first by economic concerns (W.W. Rostow), followed by political ones with the theory of the centre and the periphery (Immanuel Wallerstein, Gunnar Myrdal, Samir Amin, Charles Bettelheim, Andre Gunder

Frank), then anthropological ones, and finally economic ones again, with the recent restructurings of 'global' capitalism. During the 'anthropological' phase, a very large number of papers on development theory, based on 'micro-scale' research, were concerned with social and cultural explanations, the role of women, the study of decision-making on local level, prestige spending, the deepening of inequalities. On any level you care to examine, and notwithstanding the failure of many programmes and projects, technocratic ideology remains very powerful. Rationality is one of the great myths (in the sense of authoritative discourses) of the West, but where economic development is concerned there are numerous experts who lay claim to reason, knowledge, science, etc., without really bothering to produce any evidence. An intransigent reality seems to demonstrate that there are too many parameters in unstable equilibrium for consistent, credible forecasting. Moreover, a lot of the 'advances' based on short-term efficiency have led to an acceleration of very large-scale imbalances: global warming, desertification, pollution, etc.

8 Ethnographies and anthropology of science

The history and philosophy of science have long been objects of study, but only in the last twenty

years or so has ethnographic and anthropological
scrutiny (often combined with historical research)
been brought to bear on scientific output and its
technological applications. This diversified research
field, crucial to the comprehension of the world
we live in, has developed continuously: study of the
construction of scientific authority and the criteria
of scientificity, critique of rhetorical modes of
scientific exposition, comparative analysis of forms
of organization in scientific research, of relations
between the state, research institutes, the market,
sponsors and civil society, and of the implications
– whether philosophic, ethical, juridical or political
– of transformations brought about by scientific
discoveries.

IV INSIDE AND OUTSIDE THE FIELD OF ANTHROPOLOGY

We remarked in the introduction that anthropology
is a 'crossroads discipline', but we should add that
the exchanges are often reciprocal. The attachment
to anthropology and ethnography shown by many
sociologists undoubtedly dates from the late 1950s
when the Chicago sociologists, influenced by Robert
Park, started to emphasize observation and research
conducted in the field. They were followed by
sociologists at the University of San Diego, then by

others across the world, in particular those known as 'interactionists' and 'ethno-methodologists'. Let us establish clearly that this is not a matter of opposition between microsociology (which can be close to anthropology) and macrosociology. Sociology and anthropology have to envisage different scales: detailed study of local configurations does not contradict structural logics on a larger scale. Of all the human sciences, history is closest to anthropology and has been most inspired by anthropological approaches. Many historians are assiduous readers of the classics of anthropology and have made very good use of them; others have drifted in that direction, so to speak 'naturally', without any obvious question of borrowing or interdisciplinarity. In France, for example, the wish to replace in their context the quantitative surveys carried out by the École des Annales led historians to take cultural factors into account. This anthropological interest shown by historians – whether spontaneous or borrowed is neither here nor there – resulted in the appearance of new objects of study: theory of the self, construction of identity, kinship structures, history of the body and bodily habits, of sexuality and the family, of the social construction of gender, of taste, of consumption practices, of housing, of the influence of art on sentiments. The study of exotic systems of thought has thrown new light on the

influence exercised by Christian theology and the art
stemming from it on ideals, body language, attitudes,
etc. Periodization (what is an epoch, a moment, a
turning point, a conjuncture, a cycle, a calendar?) is
evidently an essential common theme of history and
anthropology, as are the notions of culture, mentality, ideology and imagination. Reflection by historians on the selection of objects of memory (rite,
monument, commemoration, archive, calendar) has
very obviously been fuelled by anthropological culture. Since Morgan's pioneering work, the study of
kinship systems has thrown up a dialogue between
anthropologists and historians of antiquity. The
ritual treatment of African sculptures or Pacific
ancestral effigies helps us to understand the role
of effigies in the funeral ceremonies of European
kings. An anthropological approach has developed
more specifically in ancient Greek studies, touching
on the notions of gods, idols, myths and beliefs, as
well as those of space, culture and politics. On the
question of the construction of a territory, a Greek
case illuminates a West African model and vice versa.
Similarly, the status of the foreigner is comparable
in the Mandingo world and ancient Greece. Anthropologists, whether Africanists, Americanists or Pacific
specialists, feel touched by Greek realities as analysed
by the more anthropological Hellenists. This seems
to them familiar territory, doubtless partly because

of the structural similarities displayed by polytheist systems of representation, but also because of a convergence in the two approaches and in the construction of research objects. A 'new new history' (no new wave is ever the last) has appeared, one that has a qualitative outlook very close to anthropology. It is based on analysis of individual experiences, is interested in the social construction of sexual roles, studies the methodological problems posed by biography, life-stories and testimony, is interested in 'conversion into narrative' and the editing involved in description. While many historians have conducted genuinely ethnographic studies, viewing history from the starting-point of the present, quite a number of ethnologists have moved in the opposite direction by perceiving the need to view their objects of study from a historical perspective. A 'big' anthropological question – for example, the transformation of gender difference into hierarchy – must inevitably lead to an interest in ancient sources on the scale of all humanity. Even when thinking very empirically, no 'field' can be conceived solely as a synchronous object, for it is also necessarily historical. The functionalist authors, in reaction to evolutionist speculations in the late nineteenth century, had undertaken to study every society as a specific configuration, but it soon became clear that history could not be left out. The principle of integration applying to any social unit of any sort is never free from contradiction, and all social practices, all models of behaviour, are subject to a perpetual movement of transformation. It was ever thus, but there can be no doubt at all that historical movements are accelerating. While less than five per cent of Africans lived in towns in 1900, more than half of them do now. The new objects of anthropology, for example migration, refugees, cosmopolitanism, new religions and the sociology of networks, are very clearly historical in nature and of pressing interest to the political sciences. With hindsight, it now appears that this diachronic dimension was underestimated by generations of authors engaged in inventorizing traditions. Reflections on frontiers, ethnicity, the nation, the state, the notion of foreigner, conflict and war similarly engage a number of disciplines: history, demography, linguistics, geography, political science and anthropology. Historians, moreover, were the first to follow up in France the innovative work of the anthropologist Frederick Barth, who forcefully pointed out that cultural identity was not so much content or substance as a relationship between groups. Other convergences are appearing between anthropology and historical and cultural geography as focused on housing, place, landscape and space. The growing interest being shown by authors in the image, and its relation to language, is also to be noted among historians as well as anthropologists. The history of art, which often claims to use an anthropological approach, is today of increasing interest to anthropologists, both disciplines being confronted by the problem of meaning and the handling of clues.

While the difference between societies with oral traditions and societies with writing should not be exaggerated, or even seen as an absolutely clear distinction, writing certainly facilitated the exercise of analytical thought and the control of large populations by an administration. Moreover, the advent of educational systems based on writing, in place of the use of images and sound, transformed the laws of cultural transmission so profoundly that we now find it difficult to imagine the modalities of such transmission without the aid of writing techniques. Orality and ritual are nevertheless getting their own back even in modern society. Studies of the media talk about 'ceremonial television', 'a detour through ethnography' or 'the staging of discourse on television'. A renewal of museography may also be on the cards, with such subjects as the imagination of collectors of 'primitive' art, or such queries as 'What is a body, an object?', 'What does explaining mean?' or 'What are the discursive properties of a route?'.

3

The Field

The basic methodology of anthropology is ethnography. This is the famous 'fieldwork', in which the
researcher shares the daily life of a different culture
(remote or close), observes, records, tries to grasp
the 'indigenous point of view', and writes. Boas and
Malinowski are recognized as the founders of this
method, one working among the Indians of the
West Coast of the United States and the other with
the inhabitants of the Trobriand Islands off New
Guinea. Boas from 1886, and Malinowski in 1914,
by going off alone to investigate on the spot instead
of speculating on the basis of tales told by explorers,
travellers, soldiers and missionaries, ushered in a
new phase of the discipline based on *monographs*:
meticulous descriptions, as complete as possible, of
the local realities. They also added to the romantic
image of the ethnographer dedicatedly describing
strange customs in far-off lands. The word 'field',
which designates both a place and an object of

research, has become a key word in anthropological circles: you are 'in the field' or 'just back from the field', you 'have your first experience of the field', you keep 'in touch with the field', and so on.

The effectiveness of field research undoubtedly lies more in a sort of spontaneous learning process than in the conscious and active side of the project. That is why, although it is important to take methodology seriously, the 'art' (as it is sometimes called) of field-work cannot be learned from books. When we are immersed in a culture different from our own, it informs and shapes us a good deal more profoundly than our conscious, organized memory allows us to understand. It resonates in us more than we reason on it. This is called learning by familiarization or 'osmosis': knowledge that hardly surfaces in the conscious mind but gives the private impression that we know the script of the events going on around us. Experience teaches us to say what is going to happen, to take into account the implicit rules of a culture. It is this slow and patient familiarization with the field that protects anthropologists against being totally at the mercy of diverse phenomena: they learn to discriminate between information and circumstantial rumour. The ordeal of the field – as we say after Freud, the ordeal of reality – is what teaches anthropologists not to waste effort on arbitrary creations, not to project onto a social

reality what they would like to see there, not to
favour their own subjective interests or those of their
privileged informants. In the quest for objectivity,
the anthropologist must struggle against two opposing tendencies. The first is to give free rein to the
organizing power of habit, trivializing impressions
from outside by slotting them into the ready-made
categories of the researcher's own intellectual heritage. The second is to define the research task as
the collection of differences, and thus to see any
information from outside the anthropologist's native
group as a sign of intrinsic foreignness. This carries
the risk of constant over-interpretation. In every
case the researcher should remain aware of the fact
that to collect a piece of information is not just to
synthesize sensitive facts, but also to modify them.
Asking an 'informant' to formulate an explanation
(a gloss) out of diverse indices like ritual practices,
everyday behaviour, the symbolic connections offered
by proverbs, aphorisms, prayers and etymologies, is
not 'gathering' but constructing a representation
which most probably did not pre-exist in that
form. One has to distinguish between the rule as
a theoretical hypothesis of the researcher and the
rule as a theoretical hypothesis of his interlocutors,
bearing in mind that the rule that actually governs
the behaviour being observed may be yet another,
different from either. The ethnographer must also

struggle against the temptation to extrapolate from the statements of a single individual who he or she wants to believe is representative of a whole culture. Especially as, once 'professionalized', an informant may eagerly embrace this role of cultural attaché. The researcher should favour raw recordings of the spontaneous sayings of individuals in action over standardized questionnaires, which have the disadvantage of formatting the answers. Like the utterances of a patient in psychoanalysis, what the informant says fills out the picture sketched by the anthropologist. He knows, after Durkheim, that the work of collecting data must be subordinated to the theoretical construct of his research object. Reality, in fact, is not given, but constructed by the researcher. Our perception is itself creative, through excess and by default: through excess because it may exaggerate certain features; by default because it selects the impressions that best correspond to our ideas. 'The testimony of the senses is itself another operation of the mind, in which conviction creates obviousness', wrote Marcel Proust in *La Prisonnière* (1923). That is why properly-trained researchers will strive to question their own classifications, their own editing of reality, to ensure that they are not themselves creating the objects they purport to study. This exercise in deconstruction, of which Claude Lévi-Strauss's *Le totémisme aujourd'hui*

$(1962)^6$ gives a precursory example, has been part of the professional knowhow for twenty years, but it was slow to take root in the face of existing empiricist and positivist a priori. Only by struggling against their own automatisms, by putting them to the test, can ethnographers buttress their descriptions. They will therefore strive to adopt as many viewpoints as possible, without claiming, however, to have assimilated the object in its totality.

In the field, anthropologists have constantly to grapple with themes and concerns that coincide neither with the categories of their own culture nor with the academic requirements of the profession. It is a most useful talent to be receptive to these. The informants for their part, placed in the position of the 'knowing' person, attribute to the 'scientist' a kind of learning that they try to understand. The information they supply is written by the anthropologist into a text of which they know little or nothing. While 'the one who knows' may not say everything he knows, the knowledge he yields is in a sense taken from him. So quite often, so-called ethnographic data are constructed out of the tension between the said and the unsaid, on the basis of the knowledge each of the two parties attributes to the other. That is why anthropologists have to keep listening. They need

6. Totemism today (Tr.)

to create a space in which the informants' values can be expressed, but also their questions and doubts. During its scientistic phase, ethnography did not always recognize the informant as a real interlocutor. The nuance is an important one, for the very term 'informant' depersonalizes the intersubjective experience of field research.

While the exclusive use of the questionnaire (standard battery interview) is to be condemned, it would be going too far to assert that there is nothing to be learned by this method. The pedagogic effort deployed by an individual (qualified or not) to explain a usage, a practice or a representation to a foreigner results in a composite product, but one that is not devoid of all meaning. The ability to explain oneself is a human specificity which it would be wrong to ignore. For all these reasons, at the beginning of a study, a long stay in the field seems desirable. It can provide a grounding by osmosis in the local mores, language, habits and customs. Independently of the deliberate conduct of the study (question-answer interviews, conversations, note-taking, recordings, etc.), the non-verbal aspects of the ethnographer's assimilation of the social codes should not be neglected: rules of precedence, attitudes, body language, mimicry, silences, laughter, interjections and so on. Friendships established with one or more receptive families forge solid links that become still stronger in the course of later, increasingly fruitful visits. An anthropologist is in the situation of a student who, having arrived to study (for example) the concepts of evil and misfortune among the Australian Aborigines, will be drawn into mastering, at the cost of prolonged effort, the complexities of clan organization and the naming process for the clans and generations. One who sets out to study mothering among the Bidjago islanders of Guinea-Bissau may end by being forced to take an interest in the possession of women by the spirits of defunct males.

During the 1970s, these efforts to decipher social reality from the inside led to a re-examination of the 'field' experience on the epistemological level. This self-exploration by the researcher was soon to be called reflexivity, a critical dimension that today seems a fundamental principle of transcultural analysis. The elimination of all reference to the investigator's role during the writing stage of the classics of anthropology was criticized as a distortion, aimed at masking the intersubjective nature of anthropological knowledge with a covering of highly abstract reasoning. Close reading of these texts reveals, however, that the factor was not so much censored as unnoticed by much of the profession. The 1960s had seen the multiplication of writings on field research, with a number of authors underlining the unique character of an experience in which the observer is his or her own research tool.

> Of all the sciences, it [anthropology] is surely alone in making the most intimate subjectivity into a means of objective demonstration... In the ethnographic experience, consequently, the observer sees himself as his own observation instrument; obviously he must learn to know himself, to obtain from one self, perceived as other by the ego using it, an evaluation that will become an integral part of the observation of other selves. Every ethnographic career finds its principle in 'confessions', whether written down or unadmitted.[7]

Anthropology jostles the scenery of established truths, for during their period in the field researchers are forced to step outside the protection of conformity to a particular world order. They witness, participate in and record the different attempts, made by human beings here and there, to make a living from the world and give it meaning. For its practitioners, the field experience provokes a double – but salutary – discomfort. The material one in the first place, which helps them to understand

7. Claude Lévi-Strauss (1960), repeated in *Anthropologie structurale* II (1973), pp. 25 and 48.

that no pre-existing definition of what comprises 'a normal life' goes without saying. After that, the more hazardous one of being obliged to tear up the tissue of habits and ready-made ideas which have protected them hitherto. The difference between an ivory-tower thinker and a field researcher is that the latter feels personally changed by the experience. One might say that anthropologists, at least those with long experience of fieldwork, are beneficiaries of linguistic and cultural 'interference'. In any case they are the main specialists in it, in a way suggested by this remark of Brecht's: 'He thought in other minds, and in his own, other minds were thinking. That is what real thought is.' The beauty of this quotation lies in its complexity, for in this context what should be understood by real thought is an interactive thought, one that has survived the ordeal of the other. Some anthropologists are primarily interested not in an external research object, but in the anthropological experience as a form of awareness produced by the meeting of two cultures. The aim of their research would seem to be a study of the self, an enrichment of self-awareness that may also, should the occasion arise, have something to say about the systems involved.

This sense of displacement can arise in fields geographically close to the ethnographer's own home, if he lives in the field for the whole duration of the

study, but will lose its subversive power if he only visits
it at intervals for research sessions. The urban field
displays specific constraints of its own. Paradoxically
perhaps, it is too easy to reach, so that the researcher
can go there often but not stay long. Apart from that,
he may find it almost impossible to keep in touch (for
example) with all the members of a family, owing to
the diversity of movements and activities. The value
set by anthropologists on experience of remote fields
as an initiation rite has been derided, especially by
critics who have never tried it. It remains nevertheless
an essential experience, for, in the absence of this
formative ordeal, one's reading and evaluation of
other people's ethnography is likely to be blunted.
The field diary, which is not written for publication,
is a precious source to the historian, but one that
should be read with perspicacity. It usually catalogues
blunders and problems of communication; it should
also list the successes, but these are more difficult
to write down. Even in remote contexts, once past
the language obstacle, anthropologists very often
notice that they can understand most of their hosts'
reactions; but this is not always something they
consider worth recording.

Study of the practice of anthropology in its historical context ('postcolonial studies') has thrown
light on the political dimension associated with the
role of the anthropologist as an heir of colonialism.

Even though the anthropologist may be a penniless
student, even though he or she may feel close emp-
athy with the people whose way of life is being
studied, to them the researcher occupies a place
apart: a symbol of modernity, of the city, of a privileged world whose citizens have the means to travel
for mysterious reasons. Field research however has
seldom been easy, and the image of the ethnographer
as a master-figure is devoid of general validity.
One has to have practised field research to be able
to talk about this with a measure of humility. The
master-figure cliché owes a great deal to the rarity
of reflexive texts admitting to the ethnographer's
impotence. It is appropriate in this context to give
all due credit as an anthropologist to Michel Leiris,
who felt strongly that the political context and the
investigator's attitude to his field ought to count as
part of the ethnographic data. In this connection
L'Afrique fantôme (1934),[8] the diary of the highly
colonial Dakar-Djibouti expedition, is especially
interesting, as Leiris deliberately published it to the
great fury of the expedition's leader, who feared
that its unflattering depiction of ethnographers and
colonial administrators might end by depriving the
former of much-valued logistical support. The day-
to-day research notes, especially those covering the

8 Phantom Africa or Ghostly Africa (Tr.)

91

Ethiopians in Gondar province, show how rarely the ethnographer can call the shots. Nevertheless, he or she exercises a symbolic power: that of describing the other, transposing personal experience into written text. And as a matter of fact it is still usually the colonizer or his descendant who does the describing, and the colonized or his descendant who is described.

In addressing cultural difference, the anthropologist also throws light on the basis of concepts specific to his own culture. By way of examples, we can cite works as different as Louis Dumont's Indian journey (from *Homo hierarchicus* in 1967 to *Homo aequalis* in 1976) and Pierre Bourdieu's study *La distinction* (1979). The movement back and forth between other and same, between them and us, makes it possible to identify what would otherwise seem so 'obvious' that the question of its relative nature would not even occur to us. The exchange aspect, the contractual character of field research, has often been emphasized. Apart from the gifts and payments which are always involved on one level or another, especially where the difference in wealth is very marked, the ethnographer may sometimes be 'hijacked' for use in local strategies. It can often be quite difficult to maintain neutrality. The hassles experienced by the ethnographer in the course of the study *are* the study, for they throw up issues unforeseen at the start and help reveal how a society or social group really functions. In France, well before the deconstructivist blizzard, Gérard Althabe chose (in contrast to Claude Lévi-Strauss) to abandon distance as a method both in his work on new towns and in his teaching, and instead undertook to use his own presence as a researcher as an investigative method. Some of the anthropologist's fields are more likely than others to invite or even compel the researcher to take a committed moral, social or political stand. Consider in particular studies on physical, moral or social suffering; consider studies among AIDS sufferers, alcoholics, the homeless, prisoners. It would be wrong – let us repeat it – to see applied anthropology as being somehow less 'noble' than fundamental research. If anthropology claims to know something about certain aspects of the contemporary world, it is only to be expected that decision-makers (those responsible for health, the economy, agricultural development, national assistance, and so on) will try to use its services.

The concept of the field as an experimental laboratory or reservation is today being contested by thinkers specializing in globalization and cultural mobility. Movements of population are accelerating. Work in the field now tends to involve improvised ad hoc networks able to follow the movements of contemporary diasporas. The 'field' is changing: refugee

camps, virtual communities, are being studied; research is now conducted both in the country of
origin and the country of settlement of dispersed
'communities' like the Paris Chinese or Brooklyn
Haitians. For a Western-educated anthropologist
from a Southern country, visiting the 'field' does not
necessarily mean venturing into *terra incognita*: it may
mean going home.

While it is not unreasonable to regard field research as the primary condition for anthropological
work, it should not be seen as offering a complete
answer. Everyone who attempts to answer the question
'What is humanity?' is practising anthropology in
one way or another. A long list of thinkers, from
Kant to Todorov, have things to say on the subject
without ever having done any fieldwork. Marcel
Mauss was not a field man either, but through his
erudition and brilliant intuitions he has exercised,
and still exercises, a lasting influence on the ideas of
anthropology. Indeed, knowing as he did the degree
of meticulousness needed to make valid observations,
he was in fact a very good teacher of investigative
methods. It should be noted that although the fact
of travelling and meeting 'people' face to face can
suggest the empirical existence of an enclosed *field*,
no anthropologist can fix the final outlines of a
culture or of a *field*. A study is not just the description
of what happens in the place where it is conducted;

it cannot reasonably ignore the role of external determinants, often studied by other specialists including geographers, demographers, historians, linguists, psychologists, etc.

4

Reading

While it is generally recognized that the social
sciences cannot be evaluated by the same criteria
of verification and refutation as the experimental
sciences, the question of truth nevertheless arises,
and that is why anthropology and philosophy
cannot avoid confronting and using each other.
The members of a given society understand one
another and understand their social world. So
they deploy a certain kind of knowledge, based on
acquired dispositions, thought patterns, experiences
and information, and apply it to their personal
situations. The methods they use are thus situated
at the point of crossover between the collective and
the individual. The anthropologist's agenda in the
field consists of trying to decipher these methods
by observing behaviour and analysing discourse. His
effort to understand is not of exactly the same nature
as that of the protagonists themselves, because he
compares his rough notes with an accumulated

learning, stored in the *literature,* that concerns other social forms in different times and places. The anthropologist's job is not limited to adventure in the field trying to understand societies from the inside, for the researcher travels with a whole library in his head. As we have seen, he must therefore manage a measure of tension between his dialogue with interlocutors in the field and the more abstract one he is conducting with 'his' authors. Each time, he is faced with the difficult exercise of trying, on the one hand, to prevent what he already knows from stifling his experiences in the field, and on the other, refining his curiosity by keeping in touch with anthropological culture. It is this exercise, practised over a significant length of time, that distinguishes 'fieldwork' from reportage.

Over the last twenty years or so, a lot of authors have been examining the curious literary genre that is ethnography. In general they have favoured explanations based on the colonial context, then the postcolonial one. Obviously this elucidation has been needed; however, the sort of neofunctionalism that interprets everything as a symptom of the period should be treated with suspicion. To explain a work exclusively in terms of its historical and cultural conditions of production is to risk running onto the rocks of absolute determinism. It is an oversimplification to view the works of Bronislaw

Malinovski, Alfred R. Radcliffe-Brown or Margaret Mead as being entirely explicable in terms of their context, or as saying more about these authors than about the subjects they were trying to address. Every researcher is located and determined by his or her own culture, but this is exactly what they try to free themselves from, by engaging in dialogue with authors from other times, other places and other disciplinary fields. What a person observes from a particular point of view cannot be explained entirely by reference to the historical conditions making that point of view possible. If some truths did not survive such radical contextualization, the exercise of ethnographic description would not be worth the effort involved. As Jürgen Habermas says in effect, great thinkers wear the garments of their time, but their thought is that of all time. Of course the classics of anthropology have aged and make us relive the time of writing when we read them; but they also tell us something about the human condition over and above any local determinisms, and the situation that brought them into being. Reading them is not always an easy exercise, for scientific progress is not consistent or linear, and one has to be careful to avoid misinterpretations resulting from the passage of time. This factor compels us to attempt a double reading: running through the text in the cultural context of its time, but also reading it in the way we can today, measured against subsequently acquired knowledge. Let us take two examples. One cannot understand a book on anthropology published before 1920 without bearing in mind the debate on evolution that had raged since the publication of Darwin's *On the Origin of Species* in 1859. One cannot understand the sometimes excessive character of the American culturalist tendency without bearing in mind its commitment to contesting the dominant racism of the period. These authors were trying to demonstrate that the diversity of human behaviour resulted not from biology but from cultural determinisms. The movement, sometimes also called 'culture and personality', is embodied in the work of Ruth Benedict, Margaret Mead, Ralph Linton and Abram Kardiner, and marked the second quarter of the twentieth century with its comparative approach and openness to other disciplines, even though these authors have been criticized for trying a little too hard.

One should read, but also re-read: how many Marxes, Nietzsches and Webers are there, after all? As many as their readers perhaps. In a discipline like anthropology it is important to go back to the text, and not to be content with summaries of summaries. Unsuspected riches lie hidden in the work of Radin, Devereux, Bateson, Leiris, and many others. Proper reading will reveal for example that Boas and Lowie did not really consider in any way that custom imposed stereotyped behaviour; and that Durkheim, whose theories are often presented as ahistorical, regarded history and sociology as two different angles on the same reality. For an anthropologist, reading plays a fundamental educational role in instilling a professional culture, an assemblage of learning, predispositions of an ethical sort, values and practical principles. So on opening a book on anthropology no one should be content with thinking: 'It's well written! It's badly written! It's jargonizing, it's hard to understand!' One should ask oneself such things as: how the book is structured, how the author develops his or her argument, what techniques of persuasion are used, whether the data could be interpreted differently, and so on.

5

Writing

Like other specialists in the human sciences, anthropologists are authors and ought therefore to
question themselves on the language they use and
their writing. Their science, if science it is, reposes
essentially on theoretical construction, based on
information; information that is itself mediated by
language. We know that everyday language carries
traditions of thought that, without most of its users
being aware of it, condition their outlook, their
conception of the world, the way they edit reality.
All debate on whether it is possible to enunciate the
truth, or truths, therefore raises these questions of
language and writing. Anthropologists have coined
a large number of neologisms to give words a more
technical meaning and avoid the fogginess of
common usage. The accumulation of this specialized
vocabulary has not resulted in real consensus, but
at least specialists can understand one another on
what is at stake in arguments over this concept or

that. Until the 1980s, few anthropologists really questioned the idea of a stable, external reality that could be discovered gradually. The Durkheimian school had opposed the empiricism of the positivist philosophies; it knew that the scientist had to construct his research object; but it had not brought critical scrutiny to bear on a writing style borrowed from nineteenth-century literary realism. Sociology and anthropology having been constructed in the logic of a break with subjectivism, the writing strove for neutrality, impartiality, even a certain impersonality. But apart from a handful of pioneers, it was not until after 1980 that anthropologists, or their commentators, confronted the crucial issue of the mode of exposition of research results. American anthropology and the multidisciplinary research carried out under the banner of 'cultural studies' played a leading role in criticizing the narrative conventions of ethnography. The recognition that writing does not go without saying – that it is problematic by definition – was not without effect on ways of seeing and defining the human sciences.

Every style postulates a theory (a general conception of the subject matter), an intellectual heritage (the 'literature') and an ethical commitment (not to judge, but to understand). Little by little, studies touching on the conditions of production of scientific knowledge, the questioning of certainties, have rehabilitated the account of lived experience, to the detriment of broad-scale theories. Today, anthropologists strive to explain the stages through which they have arrived at what they think. They try to make explicit their shuttling back and forth between theory and 'field'. The work is no longer a matter of overflying the experience of the actors at high altitude, but of restoring the located and interactive character of ethnography. Their texts give more space to other voices than to the researcher's own: voices from the archives, those of interlocutors in the field, of philosophers, literary theorists, writers. Closer attention is given to social interactions, to the anthropology of speech and other modes of communication. It is accepted, in effect, that every statement relates to a context, is contingent on the personalities of the researcher and the informants, is subject to variations caused by a wide range of factors. And these days, the authors of anthropological texts are more likely than ever before to have to explain themselves; their divine right to exercise total control over their own narrative is being contested. We no longer believe that an individual 'represents' his culture fully, that he is somehow its metonymy, a representative sample of it in all his thoughts and actions. And we now seek to diversify our sources, to treat official discourse with reserve, to take note of the women's point of view, to give full attention to the weak or the ruled. The idea that 'simple' or 'limited' societies are consensual has faded progressively as field studies have become more exact and specific. So anthropological writing should stop trying to melt all this diversity together into an abstract unity and do the opposite: respect the diversity and reflect it. The form of the text synchronizes easily with the tentative rhythm of the research itself: the object is to establish a truth about humanity through whatever knowledge is exchanged while surmounting or avoiding the pitfalls of ethnocentric partiality. Reflexivity – the researcher's scrutiny brought to bear on himself, the attempt to objectivize his own subjectivity – has become a main requirement of research. The monograph, as an ostensibly exhaustive description of a localized society, is the representative form par excellence of the classical age of anthropology (running more or less from 1920 to 1975). Since then, numerous texts have attempted to place local observation in the context of an acceleration of history and of globalization. The monograph has not disappeared, however; on the contrary, more are being published than ever before. But the essay is more fashionable these days. The essay – an argued point of view on a theme – tries to compare local realities with truths on a larger spatial and/or temporal scale. But it would be wrong to see this as a recent innovation: Marcel Mauss's

Essai sur le don (1925)[9] is one masterly example of it. Questions on the relationship between language and reality will surely continue to fuel philosophic debate. Perhaps one day the cognitive sciences will manage to produce a genuinely scientific answer. In the meantime, anthropology cannot usefully validate its methods by conducting *fewer* field studies and writing *fewer* descriptions. Nevertheless, given the growing presence of the uncertainty principle, linear and continuous narrative may well give more ground to montage effects. New kinds of writing will emerge, giving more space to the dialogue between author and 'subjects' and between author and readers. Too many anthropologists continue to behave as if the 'subjects' of their descriptions were 'unlettered' by definition, when in reality the work of researchers is becoming ever more accessible to them, and they may have well-formulated advice, opinions and criticisms of their own. Anthropology will also be multidisciplinary, adding to its own outlook those of the other human sciences and literature with which it is already 'in conversation'. Anthropology needs philosophy, psychology, psychoanalysis, linguistics, the political sciences, economics, geography and history, and already engages in public debates with journalists, writers, film-makers and artists. The great

9. 'Essay on the gift' or 'Essay on giving' (Tr.)

traumas of recent history (Holocaust, mass crimes of the Khmer Rouge, Rwandan genocide, etc.) have given rise to literary works and films that are interesting to anthropologists not only as sources, but often also for their theoretical outlook and mode of exposition. Techniques other than writing, most notably cinema and video, hold out the possibility of 'conveying' an atmosphere or ambiance, allowing people to speak, interaction, following the progress of an action. No one should imagine, however, that this is a 'transparent' medium, able to recreate events without mediation. 'Reality effects', as Roland Barthes calls them, are no easier to produce in cinema than they are in literature. In both cases, what we are dealing with is a constructed discourse.

6

Avoiding Blind Alleys

The human sciences subject their hypotheses, concepts, methods and writing styles to perpetual reassessment. In the course of their history, it seems, they have oscillated between two poles: at one extreme a desire for rootedness, foundation and order; at the other, scepticism and deconstruction, a sort of romanticism. Oversimplified bipolar contrasts – order/disorder, collective/individual, objective/ subjective, meaning/function – have severely limited the productivity of any hypotheses by imprisoning theoretical reflection in a series of dilemmas. Sociology and anthropology were both constructed in defiance of subjective intuition by adopting a *holistic* approach, seeking to identify the relations that lie at the basis of a system.

Some twenty years ago this holism inherited from Henri Maine, Ferdinand Tönnies and Émile Durkheim, which studied the general norms of a society to explain the behaviour of individuals, gave way to a methodological individualism inherited from Max Weber, which starts with the individual actor and tries to understand why he acts as he does. From this angle, the society or institution is seen as the result of social interactions; norms are the product of these interactions, not the cause. One of the problems that face an anthropologist, when trying to interpret patterns which seem to contain the makings of a model, is whether there is a pre-existing prescriptive structure (an institution) that sets behavioural norms, or whether the structure is produced by the interplay of practices. What we are confronted with here, in fact, is an example of reciprocal implication: the individual is produced by society, but society can only be produced by individuals. To posit an opposition between the individual and society is therefore absurd in the sense that the individual cannot think of himself in isolation and inevitably embodies aspects of the collective. On the scale of order/disorder, the present period leans somewhat towards the disorder pole, just as it values doubt more than certainty and the particular more than the general. Critical texts recognize the chaotic character of the world and the implosion of the grand narratives. Recent published works have relentlessly underlined the 'fictional' nature of the general notions of evolutionist, diffusionist, functionalist and structuralist anthropologists, and those who have followed them. Without wishing to get entangled in some endless squabble over words, we would point out that it is not very interesting to declare that everything is fiction and fiction is in everything. It is a truism that every text is a construction; but to assert that a text from one of the human sciences is a fiction, merely because it does not claim to contain the definitive truth, is an abuse of language or at best a rhetorical flourish. It is sensible in practice to draw careful distinctions between fiction, error, lie, fake, ideological argument, model, hypothesis, and so on. In fiction, the author consciously and deliberately sets out with the intention of inventing: what he or she offers the reader is the ingenuity of an invented story. The story may be inspired by reality, but the referent is clearly identified as imaginary, and the central events described have not occurred historically. The great nineteenth-century evolutionists, men like Tylor, Morgan and Frazer, saw themselves quite sincerely as a new breed of historians of civilization. They saw different human societies as representing stages on the path of a single, linear progression, as if the final purpose of the whole of humanity were to engender Western society. That they were wrong, that they were influenced by Western chauvinism, is undeniable, but being mistaken is not the same thing as writing a work of fiction. Similarly, some late nineteenth-century anthropologists, on noting the

extraordinary morphological resemblance between
human institutions in parts of the world widely
separated in space and time – artisanal techniques,
forms of housing, kinship structures, funeral rites,
song and dance, rituals, everything from agrarian
practices to conventions of warfare – tried their best
to study the geographical distribution of cultural
characteristics and retrace the map of their diffusion.
The problem here is that the diffusionists, just like the
evolutionists, showed little discernment in judging
the reliability of the sources they used to corroborate
their preconceived theory. The word functionalism
these days is almost a pejorative, for we know that the
constituent parts of a society do not 'function' like
the parts of a machine or the organs of a living being,
but Radcliffe-Brown's structure was the model of the
conduct of relations between individuals, a model
he sincerely believed to be inherent in the observed
data. Later, some authors criticized structuralism
for postulating a fixed relation between signifier
and signified, but that was a hypothesis formulated
in the context of a general theory of signs. In this
respect structuralism had a profound effect on the
way anthropology is conducted, even though its
extreme forms, reducing the whole of social life to a
semiology, have been resisted.

Anthropological analysis is necessarily structural,
comparative and more general in scope than the

simple reporting of particular cases. There are also ontological a priori that posit opposition between representations and practices, between meaning and function. Symbolic systems are only effective to the extent that they both signify and function at the same time. In order to act on the world one has to attribute meaning to it; so the deployment of social logics needs to be analysed, as well as their structure. Feminist anthropologists demonstrated, from 1970 onward, that the conceptions of the world projected by the classics of anthropology nearly always embodied a male point of view. It is certainly reasonable, in this connection, to talk of a bias or prejudice that contemporary anthropology is in a position to correct. Similarly, one cannot reasonably compare the reality of local particularities with the fiction of universals postulated once and for all by the scientist. The ultimate aim of anthropology is to explain the variability of human acts, and the study of this variability necessarily also includes the variability of resemblances and of universals. If the diversity of specific descriptions, taken from a history which is in continuous movement and perpetually redistributes roles, made all generalization and all comparison impossible, anthropology would not be much use. It can happen, of course, that the assertion of patterns and invariables rests on an author's skill in marshalling a large amount of factual information

in support of a general idea, but it is not always like
that. Any and every argued hypothesis is subject
to debate between professionals, in the setting of
what Habermas calls an ideal speech situation: one
in which the quest for truth is the sole objective. It
is this debate, based on a very close reading of the
texts and on comparison, that enables the work of
an anthropologist or ethnographer to be evaluated.
The raw materials of a piece of research may well
be deemed artefacts produced by the researcher
rather than givens, but it may also be admitted that
some part of the external reality comes through
the specificities of the study. No doubt all scientific
theories are stories or narratives up to a point, but
they are not stories in the usual sense. It is pernicious
to set narratives produced for entertainment,
advertising, propaganda or proselytizing purposes on
the same level as those aiming to produce objective
knowledge. The fact that knowledge is only accessible
through the prism of a particular culture does not
make reality as an object disappear, nor does it
eliminate the universal scope of any discoveries. The
dismantling of inventions and constructs demystifies
belief in a certain definition of reality; it does not
prove that there is no reality. The theoreticians of
deconstruction are eager to label as fictions a range
of quite complex entities: society, social system,
social organization, social structure, culture, the

French, etc. All the same, authors who strive to eliminate these words from their vocabulary, along with
all the biological and mechanistic metaphors that
accompany them, are obliged, when they need to
depart from the individual level, to resort to terms
that are just as global or even more so: the world
of something, the universe of something, the 'some-
thingsphere'. Whereas, while they should certainly be
subjected to close examination, holistic notions like
the institutional mind (Montesquieu), the objective
mind (Hegel), the signifying whole (Dilthey),
collective consciousness (Durkheim), the ideal type
(Weber), symbolic systems (Lévi-Strauss), the imaginary institution (Castoriadis), ideo-logic (Augé)
and 'the mental and the material' (Godelier) are
useful concepts, the sort of things that can help us
understand the social bond. In reality, holism and
individualism are not alternatives that can be ranked
on a scale of true or false; they are methodological
choices each of which offers advantages and draw-
backs. The same society can be studied from different
points of view, for example the Pathans of Pakistan's
North-West frontier, by Fredrik Barth on the basis
of the individual and games theory, and by A. Assad
in terms of a systemic theory inspired by Marxism.
These are two different forms of illumination thrown
on the same object, two models whose pertinence
can be discussed.

To suggest an opposition between the inductive and deductive approaches would start a bad quarrel, for a proper anthropologist must obviously make use of both. He immerses himself in a local reality, observes, participates, describes, records, films, and so on, until a model emerges (this is the inductive approach); but he also constantly tests theoretical hypotheses (his own and those of his interlocutors), corroborating or invalidating them by observing the facts. Something that complicates the construction of the image we give to others in our books and films is that we can never be quite certain of the moment when we are doing them most justice as a group and as individuals: when we are showing them as very different from ourselves, or when we are showing them as exactly the same; when we are underlining particularities, or when we are discovering the universal. The anthropologist is always subject to contradictory experiences but, while highly sensitive to differences, can also note every day that human beings all resemble each other far more than they differ. This difficult issue evidently has strong implications on the scientific, moral and political levels, but the intellectual debate is often needlessly dramatized by the over-hasty formulation of normative judgements. In this connection, classical essentialism – belief in a stable definition (with fixed properties) of a society or culture – is a much more cumbersome burden than the wish of relativists (often called postmoderns) to explain everything in terms of its historical context. The desire, associated with colonial ethnology, to classify human beings into distinct races prefigured in a sense today's emphasis on minority and community issues. In both cases the project is to extract a 'society' from its historical environment, to preserve it from the larger whole that contains it, in other words the state. In the United States, the model of the parish and the churches certainly played a role in the emergence of strong community awareness, and thus led eventually to multiculturalism. Tocqueville showed that the American churches could not compete with the state, because the separation had been established at the outset. The institutions belonging to the churches did not fall into the hands of the state, as they had in most European countries. The community mentality developing in Europe today stems from a decline in the inclusive power of the state, combined with the little-noticed spread of a sort of vulgarized anthropology tinged with moralism. In this ideology, the celebration of cultural differences serves as the a priori, in place of an understanding of the mechanisms underlying the construction of identity, and hence of otherness. Identity-asserting movements do not call for any moral judgement on the anthropologist's part.

They exist, and one has to try to explain them, to understand them. All the populations of the world are ruled by global mechanisms (movements of capital, goods, population, messages, images) which elude their understanding or control and whose structuring authority is world capitalism. Everyone, today, is 'caught' in networks, markets, exchanges, and most of us consider that we have no firm grasp of a rapidly-changing world system. It is hardly surprising, therefore, that here and there people should band together, adapt their culture to the challenges of the moment, make creative use of their past to try to find their place and secure a few advantages. The anthropologist can deconstruct these ideologies by showing that exclusivism in all its forms – racial, ethnic, class, religious, sexual, and so on – is falsely presented as essential and intrinsic, but he or she should also work as a historian to study the conditions of its emergence. To the message of the historian Eric Hobsbawm, who noted two decades ago that traditions are ceaselessly invented and reinvented, the anthropologist can add that there is no culture without politics and staging. Identity today owes as much to the global as to the local, to the expectation of survival as to the past, to the state as to the native soil: indeed, for good and ill, it is the articulation of these things.

118

Conclusion

The contrast between us and them (modern/primit-
ive; North/South; West/East) is an anthropological a
priori that has been much criticized in recent years.
Edward W. Said (*Orientalism*, 1979) and his followers
have singled out in particular the West's instrumentalization of the notion of *culture* to establish a
division between the West and the rest of the world.
Until then, intellectuals from the 'South' had tended
to concentrate their critiques on 'ethnocide' (Robert
Jaulin), meaning premeditated violence exercised by
the West to reduce all cultural differences and shape
the world in the Western image. So anthropology
finds itself attacked from both sides, accused simultaneously of assimilationism and primitivism. On the
level of values, the genesis of a division between the
West and the rest of the world is without foundation,
and the construction of a single category to cover
the whole of 'non-industrialized' humanity is absurd.
On the scientific level, however, a split between
the modern peoples and the *others* is not so easily

119

dismissed. Anthropology is the result of a complex scientific development that took place in the West in three main stages. The first of these resulted from the extraordinary surge of Greek and Roman philosophy, which laid the foundations not only of anthropology and history but also of metaphysics, aesthetics, ethics, rhetoric, mathematics, and so on. The second stage corresponds to the scientific and philosophic developments of the eighteenth-century 'Enlightenment', and the third to the period of the industrial revolution. Two major events, which undoubtedly led to radical change in the ways the world is perceived, should be taken very seriously: firstly writing and printing, neither of which is a Western discovery but which were adopted and developed in Europe; and later, the industrial revolution. Walter J. Ong, Jack Goody and others have shown that writing as a technology introduces a major transformation, bringing fundamental change to acts of communication. We have not yet examined all the implications of this revolution, either on cognitive processes, education and social control or on technological progress, the conservation of archives, cultural accumulation. The industrial revolution, based on liberalism[10] and the market

10. 'Liberalism' here means *economic* liberalism – broadly, so-called free trade – not political or moral liberalism. Politically, economic liberalism is generally associated with conservative attitudes (Tr.)

economy, also brought a decisive transformation. Evolutionism, which held that all social forms tended towards this model, has quite rightly been refuted, but one cannot avoid seeing that like it or not, the entire planet – embodied in the name of the latest phase, *globalization* – has been restructured or destructured by it. According to Karl Polanyi, this *great transformation* is creating a gulf between the *moderns* who operated this liberal revolution and all the other social forms (on this subject see Louis Dumont, *Essais sur l'individualisme*, 1983).[11] There is no doubt that this transformation is less rational than people think, that even the most 'developed' post-industrial society cannot be wholly explained without reference to the symbolic, to ideology and beliefs; but it has brought about a professionalization of scientific and technological research. This does not mean that Western societies have some sort of monopoly on critical reflection: individuals in all human societies, living through a diversity of experiences, stand back from time to time to analyse the meaning of their actions. Nowhere are human beings just cultural automata; nowhere are they reduced to exclusive roles defined once and for all. On the other hand, not all cultures have embraced a scientific model based on the confrontation of rational arguments

11. Essays on individualism (Tr.)

with the sole purpose of establishing laws, patterns, structures. What is being discussed today is whether this autonomization of science and research is introducing an epistemological break from all the other forms of knowledge, or whether the category isolated under the name 'science' is just one relative form of learning among all the rest. We do not share the historicist point of view that there exists no universal truth, but only fragmentary statements that can be wholly explained in terms of their historical and cultural context. When a discovery is made in one part of the world, it can quickly take on a universal dimension: science, today and long since, belongs to everyone.

It is difficult to map the broad lines of the profession at present, the period being characterized by a multiplicity of approaches and the proliferation of objects of study. The vast majority of output is still 'classical' (in the sense that it is 'empirical'), but critical tendencies tend to predominate in debate and occupy centre stage. Painting in very broad strokes, one might say that the empiricists continue to believe in the value of observation, are reluctant to question the 'achievements of the discipline' and (on the whole) steer clear of the epistemological arguments. From reading the debates featured in the more forward-looking reviews one might get the impression that the ethnographic monograph – fullest possible

description of a social unit – has become a thing of
the past, a little like the nineteenth-century realist
novel in literature, often declared to be moribund.
In reality this is not the case at all: just as more
realist novels are being published now than in the
nineteenth century, more monographs are being
written today than in the golden age of the monograph. Nor do the empiricists limit themselves to
description; using their field data and the resources
of the literature, they formulate theories distributed
between two poles: those that attempt to corroborate
a general hypothesis (functionalist, for example) and
those that proceed through induction, attempting
to understand large-scale sociological phenomena
through analysis of well-documented individual
cases. What with the discipline's many different sub-
fields, a very large number of texts are still published
each year on a wide variety of objects, from economic
anthropology to the relations between culture and
personality. Semiological structuralism is perhaps
practised less often these days in its canonical form,
but remains influential. Numerous approaches are
called post-structuralist today not because they reject
the notions of codes, codification and symbolic set
proposed by structuralism, but rather because they
reject an ahistorical vision, a mentalist philosophy
and a careless attitude to source materials. Interpretative (sometimes called hermeneutic) anthropology

also continues to exercise strong influence, but at the same time has fallen into an anti-positivist posture, vehemently contesting the idea that there could ever be such a thing as 'naked data'. A large number of anthropologists agree on the fact that signification is socially, historically and rhetorically constructed. On the other hand, what has been called *textualism* – viewing the meaning of what people do as a discourse, a text, which simply has to be read – has been energetically criticized. A relativist epistemology, currently very fashionable, no longer accepts scientific truth as the regulating principle for scientific practices including the individual's own research. No doubt if this became widespread it might lead to the dissolution of the discipline; however, it quite often seems to result in the conversion of researchers to philosophy or artistic activities. At the opposite pole to this extreme scepticism concerning theory is a body of research that relies heavily on an effort of theoretical rigour, starting from a meticulous study based on ethnolinguistics, sociolinguistics, anthropology of nature, with a sustained interest in orderings of the world, taxonomies, social interactions, cognitive processes. The study of cultural products or representations, both as systems of knowledge and as systems of mental predisposition, has reopened the debate between particularism and universalism. 'Postcolonial studies' and the massive and widespread critique of cultural essentialism (attributing fixed properties to a culture) have encouraged a new form of functionalism, interpreting social behaviour with reference to its background context, in terms of choices, strategies and negotiation. A current that is powerful and stimulating, but that should probably be seen in the context of the increasing difficulty of the 'field' and its problematization, turns the mirror of anthropology back on itself. The theoretical diagram borrows from causal structuralism, functionalism and Marxism, showing how the researcher's gaze is determined by the conditions of production that prevail in the discipline. Anthropologists' categories of thought, their values, the rules they follow, their relations with 'others' in the field, their archiving techniques and writing, can all be explained from the historical context and the way research as an institution is defined. In this connection it is interesting to pay attention to national traditions, not just in the countries where academic anthropology was born, but also in ones that have adapted its model. Anthropologists in Latin America receive much the same training as those in other 'Western' countries, but they undoubtedly show greater commitment than others in defence of the rights of the people they observe. The problematic of exoticism (the controversial 'them/us' contrast) is more vividly apparent there than in Europe or the United States, for the examination of difference has more immediate political implications. Exoticism exists so to speak within the national boundaries and is therefore, whatever the difficulties, a constituent of the national identity. There is a very rich Latin American and foreign literature documenting different aspects of the lives of Indian tribes: kinship, cosmology, migrations, ecology, economy, politics.

On a larger scale, a whole range of studies have examined racial prejudice, hierarchy, individualism, anthropology of towns, forms of the family, education, drugs, violence, relations between science and society, relations between psychoanalysis and anthropology, religious revivals, Afro-American cults. The specificity common to these anthropologies is an interest in the theorization of conflict, of the 'frontier', contact, 'ethnic frictions', national integration, indigenisms. We can no longer think of anthropology as the importation of the heritages of oral-transmission societies into the domain of writing. In many contexts literacy was acquired, at least partially, generations ago. Malinowski for instance, who regarded the monograph as the most valid but also the most difficult form of ethnography, had encouraged one Hsiao-Tung Fei to publish his monograph on Chinese peasants. Later, Mysore N. Srinavas published his work on the Coorgs of southern India,

126

followed by other Indian researchers of international renown. Many researchers today work in their own native communities, sometimes committed to modernization movements, sometimes maintaining a prudent distance from the mêlée. During the 1980s the expression 'indigenous anthropology' started to appear in the academic literature, designating studies conducted by researchers from minority groups. Some considerable heat has been generated by the debate: 'Should Indian or African anthropologists be anthropologists first and foremost, thinking in accordance with the conventions and academic sorting methods of the profession, or can they develop their own angles on research, without conforming slavishly to pre-established models?'. It is very probable that an anthropologist who comes from Asia, Africa or Oceania, even one with a Western education, will be especially sensitive to any traces of ethnocentrism hidden inside allegedly objective conceptualizations. It may well be thought, moreover, that the fact of belonging to two cultures is an enrichment. It is known that writers in languages other than their own, or who speak more than one language, often have peculiarities of style attributable to the phenomenon of *interference*, a word used in linguistics to designate the restructurings that result from the introduction of foreign elements. Other writings from outside the ethnographic literature can prove extremely valuable, for example the metaphysical reflections of Indian Pundits and literary works in general, writers being very acute observers of social life. The people who used to be the 'subjects' of books written by Western researchers now read those books and sometimes write new ones, which is surely a positive development. On the other hand, there are occasional signs of a somewhat obscurantist tendency that advocates restricting the right to describe and analyse to members of the 'community' concerned. This is very obviously an expression of antinomic closure from the objectives – comparativist but also universalist – of anthropology. Some authors from the 'South' advance their own vision of the northern countries, but the great imbalance between rich countries, where academic research is an established and financed branch of activity, and so-called 'emerging' ones where it is seen as a luxury, hampers this crossing of viewpoints. Indeed the means allocated to research are so unequally distributed that large numbers of researchers from Africa, Asia, Oceania and Latin America try to find refuge in Western universities and institutes. North, South, East and West, a vigorous tendency in contemporary anthropology has finally abandoned the nostalgic quest for lost paradises to concentrate on trying to understand the world as it is. The conservative view of cultural heritage, reified by the word 'tradition', has encouraged an oversimplified, antinomic conception of social change (tradition vs. modernity). We know today that there are very few places in the world that can boast an authentic autochthony, that ethnicity is more a relationship than the property of a group, that the market economy and state institutions are not incompatible with lineage-based structures, that a guerrilla movement may resort to trances and spirit possession, that 'global' exchanges – trade of every kind, migrations, transfers of goods over long distances and long periods of time – date from long before the invention of the steam engine. It is time to stop regarding anthropology as a quest for origins and lost paradises, or as a catalogue of resistances to Westernization. The role of anthropologists is not to discover unknown groups or fill the gaps in the cultural atlas; it is to propose a critical analysis of modes of cultural expression in the historical context that gives them their meaning. To that end, they should be able to assess the scale of the transformations taking place in our world (genetic engineering, information technologies, digital image) and the major challenges facing it: disparities of wealth, environmental damage, new pandemics. What is at stake for twenty-first-century anthropology concerns not the disappearance or preservation of 'traditional' societies, but relations between groups, interactions between the local reality, empirically observable in the field, and phenomena of worldwide or global reach. Ethnography, the basic methodology on which anthropology rests, can shed useful light on a world where virtual pressure groups, IT networks, flows of capital, migrants, messages and digital images increasingly permeate societies and cultures that were always fairly permeable by definition. In the frontier zone between history, anthropology and sociology, we also need to reflect on the forms of individualism now developing in Western societies. Analysis of this consumers' individualism needs to measure the full impact of the media and the weakening of institutions that carry the social bond: family, lineage, clan, state, school, and even – spectacular seizures notwithstanding – religion. Anthropology now has necessarily to work on and between different scales: local, national and 'globalized'.

The human sciences cannot dispense with a contextualized analysis of the relations between individuals in a given group. What we observe in effect, on a small or large scale, is frequent social recomposition, endless reconstructions and reassertions of identity whose political and/or religious expression, often with the help of the media, quickly becomes more or less familiar to all. The relations and the context change together, not without some apparent contradictions. The individualization of behaviour (especially consumer behaviour) is a concomitant of these recompositions of identity. The process coincides with the unprecedented development of communication technologies that change the nature of relations, and also with the extension of deterritorialized spaces in which symbols are replaced by codes. Also apparent, alongside a hardening of local contexts (particularisms of every sort), is the globalization of technologies and the economy, and what one might call the spread of a planetary consciousness. Humanity is becoming self-aware, but violence and relations of force continue to menace its future. The world is becoming more uniform, but the gulf between extremes of wealth and poverty is wider than ever. Science is making revolutionary strides in knowledge of the outer universe and the inner workings of life, but religiosity of every stripe has seldom loomed larger.

All these contradictions are there to be seen, to be read, in small-scale patterns and local events whose internal logic, external determinants and general significance the anthropological perspective is specifically tuned to understand.

Bibliography

Althabe, G. and Selim, M., *Démarches ethnologiques au présent*, Paris, L'Harmattan, 1998.

Augé, Marc, *Pour une anthropologie des mondes contemporains*, Paris, Aubier, 'Critiques', 1994.

Balandier, Georges, *Sociologie actuelle de l'Afrique noire*, Paris, PUF, 1955.

Bonte, Pierre and Izard, Michel, *Dictionnaire de l'ethnologie et de l'anthropologie*, Paris, PUF, 1991; 2nd ed., 1992; republished 'Quadrige', 2000.

Clifford, James, *Routes, Travel and Translation in the Late Twentieth Century*, Cambridge (Mass.) – London, Harvard University Press, 1997.

Evans-Pritchard, E.E., *Witchcraft, Oracles and Magic among the Azande*, London, Faber and Faber, 1937.

Geertz, Clifford, *Works and Lives: The Anthropologist as Author*, Stanford University Press, 1988.

Godelier, Maurice, *Rationalité et irrationalité en économie*, Paris, Maspéro, 1969.

133

Héritier, Françoise, *Masculin/féminin. La pensée de la différence*, Paris, Odile Jacob, 1996.

Lévi-Strauss Claude, *Anthropologie structurale* II, Paris, Plon, 1973.

Sapir, Edward, *Anthropologie*, Paris, Éditions de Minuit (First ed. 1949), 1967.